COUNSELLING SUPERVISION IN CONTEXT

Counselling Supervision

The *Counselling Supervision* series, edited by Michael Carroll and Elizabeth Holloway, has a clearly defined focus on counselling supervision issues and emphasizes the actual practice of counselling supervision, drawing on up-to-date models of supervision to assist, inform and update trainee and practising counsellors, counselling psychologists and psychotherapists.

Titles in the series include:

COUNSELLING SUPERVISION
IN CONTEXT

Edited by
Michael Carroll and Elizabeth Holloway

SAGE Publications
London • Thousand Oaks • New Delhi

First published 1999

SAGE Publications Ltd
6 Bonhill Street
London EC2A 4PU

SAGE Publications Inc
2455 Teller Road
Thousand Oaks, California 91320

SAGE Publications India Pvt Ltd
32, M-Block Market
Greater Kailash – I
New Delhi 110 048

British Library Cataloguing in Publication data

A catalogue record for this book is
available from the British Library

ISBN 0-7619-5788-X
ISBN 0-7619-5789-8 (pbk)

Library of Congress catalog card number 98–61426

Typeset by Photoprint, Torquay, Devon
Printed in Great Britain by Biddles Ltd, Guildford, Surrey

Contents

Notes on Contributors

Michael Carroll, Ph.D., is a chartered counselling psychologist and Fellow of the BAC. He has been Director of Studies in Psychology and Counselling at Roehampton Institute London and Director of Counselling and Training at Right Cavendish, London. He is consultant to a number of organizations in both the public and private spheres.

Patricia Grant, MSc (Psychological Counselling), is a United Kingdom Registered Counsellor and a BAC accredited supervisor. She works at the University of Greenwich where she is involved in teacher education as well as teaching on their MSc in Therapeutic Counselling. She has a particular interest in the part played by race and culture in counselling and supervision.

Shoshana Hellman was born in Israel and has an MA in linguistics from the Sorbonne, France and an MA, Ed.M and Ed.D in counselling psychology from Columbia University, NY. Since 1980, she has been working in Israel as a supervisor of school counsellors for the Ministry of Education, department of psychological services. She also teaches counselling and supervision courses at the university.

Penny Henderson works independently. She offers counselling, supervision of counsellors, organizational consultancy, training about communication and teamwork, and team building for organizations. She is an associate of the Counselling in Primary Care Trust and the National Institute of Social Work and contributes to the training of medical students in Cambridge.

Paul Hitchings is a chartered counselling psychologist and UKCP registered psychotherapist. He works both in private practice as a counsellor and supervisor, and also at Metanoia Institute where he teaches on a number of different programmes. His particular interests include: training and working with beginning super-visees, multi-disciplinary contributions to the work of the counsellor and on the psychology of political issues especially that of sexual orientation within the broad field of counselling psychology.

Elizabeth Holloway, Ph.D., is a professor in the Department of Counselling Psychology at the University of Wisconsin-Madison and has directed clinical training centres at the Universities of California, Oregon and Wisconsin. She is a Fellow of Division 17 (Counselling Psychology) of the American Psychological Asso-ciation and is a Diplomate in Counselling Psychology of the American Board of Professional Psychology. Elizabeth is author of *Clinical Supervision: A Systems Approach* (1995, Sage).

Elizabeth Mann is a chartered counselling psychologist who is a lecturer, therapist, supervisor and independent consultant in the management of counselling in organizations. In the religious context, she works in the UK and overseas to research, initiate and develop systems for psychological assessment, therapy and train-ing of priests and ministers.

Mary Lee Nelson, Ph.D., is an Assistant Professor of Counsellor Education and Supervision at the University of Washington in Seattle. She is a licensed psychologist and certified by the National Board of Certified Counsellors. She teaches counselling and super-vision and conducts research on supervision and gender. She has written numerous articles on gender and its relation to counselling and supervision.

Caron Oyston practices as a counsellor and supervisor in Woking, Surrey. She is an accredited member of BAC and a UK Registered Independent Counsellor. Caron lives with progressive Multiple Sclerosis and is committed to raising the awareness of other ther-apists, and supervisors, to the needs of people with disabilities.

Terri Spy, M.Sc., works as a counsellor, trainer, supervisor and psychotherapist from her practice in West Wimbledon. Terri is accredited by BAC as a counsellor, supervisor and trainer. She is also a UKCP registered integrative psychotherapist. Terri, as a practising Christian, has a commitment to equality of people regardless of race, culture, gender or ability.

Margaret Tholstrup, M.Sc., is a chartered counselling psychologist and UKCP-registered psychotherapist as well as having BAC accreditation both as a counsellor and as a group and individual supervisor. She set up the Student Counselling Service at the Roehampton Institute, London and currently divides her time between her private practice as a trainer, supervisor and psychotherapist, and counselling psychologist in a GP surgery.

John Towler, PGCEA, Dip. Hum. Psych., is a freelance counselling therapist, supervisor, facilitator and teacher, working primarily in organizational settings. Trained as a priest he has worked as director of a counselling service and senior lecturer in a tertiary college. He is a consultant for Humanitas, an Associate Lecturer for Roehampton Institute, London, and has a private practice in Hampshire.

Acknowledgements

We would like to dedicate this book to all the British supervisors who have worked so hard and diligently to bring supervision to the high level of theory and practice it enjoys today. Our particular thanks to the authors who have contributed to the book and to Susan Worsey at Sage who is, as ever, a delight to work with. Elizabeth would like to express her gratitude to the trainers in Britain who have welcomed her to their shores and taught her so much about supervision as a lifelong enterprise. Michael would like to mention Beatrice, Nigel and Sue who have been exemplars of dedicated counselling and expert supervisees.

Introduction

Michael Carroll
Elizabeth Holloway

Anne Alonso (1985) once described supervision as a 'complicated hall of mirrors'. Not only does this image capture the 'reflection process' that is part and parcel of supervision but it illustrates the many dimensions that appear when two individuals or more (supervisor and supervisee/s) contemplate what happens in work with clients. The focal points for this contemplation can be numerous: the client, the counsellor, the therapeutic relationship, the interventions employed, the supervisor, the relationship with the supervisor, the organization in which this takes place, the systemic influences on all or any of the parties involved, the training course of the supervisee, the future personal and professional development of the supervisee. Within each of these focal points there are many further dimensions that play crucial roles in the whole process of counselling and supervision. Take for instance the client. It is relatively easy to 'lump' all distinguishing features of clients together and call the end result 'the client'. To do so, however, is to do injustice to the amazing features and characteristics that go to make up individuals. The client is of a certain age, gender, race, culture. Furthermore, there may be distinguishing aspects of this person that, if overlooked, ignored or not thought important, could do immense damage to the relationship, for example disability or sexual orientation. Individual differences not only matter but are at the very heart of what it means to be a person. It is too easy for counsellors to use statements such as 'I treat all people equally', 'To me there is no such thing as colour', 'Why should it matter whether my client is gay or straight?', 'All counselling is just the same as private counselling'. Admirable though the underlying sentiments may be, from the perspective of the client these features of their lives may be paramount to who they are and why they are in counselling. To ignore them is to ignore a fundamental part of the person.

Individual clients will receive counselling in a particular setting according to their service needs and/or demographic character-istics such as age, socio-economic status, occupation and gender. The settings in which counselling takes place can greatly influence the supervision of the counsellor. Whether counselling occurs in a medical, educational, workplace or religious setting, the culture of the organization of service delivery infiltrates work with clients and thus the work of supervision. To ignore the contextual factors could cause the supervisor and counsellor alike to assume that the client is solely responsible for the problem. For example, it would be too easy for both counsellor and supervisor to assess a work-place counselling client for stress and set up individual inter-ventions to deal with the stress problem when the actual problem lies with the company which is making unreasonable demands.

One of the skills in being an effective supervisor is to have what Hawkins and Shohet (1989) called the 'helicopter' ability, that is, being able to see clients in ever widening perspectives so that they can be assessed and worked with in their full contexts. This means that the impact of different systems on their lives can be seen and understood, with the result that clients are not made responsible for what is not their problem and that interventions for change incorporate an understanding of the individual in the system.

Several authors have criticized counselling for concentrating only on the internal world of clients and making them responsible for what happens to them as if they had chosen it or brought it about. In an attack on those who would do so, Smail (1985: 76) gives a powerful image and example of how easy it is to fall into this trap: 'If you run over a pea with a steam-roller you don't blame the pea for what happens to it, nor, sensibly, do you treat its injuries as some kind of shortcoming inherent in its internal structure, whether inherited or acquired', and concomitantly, Pilgrim (1997: ix) writes:

> This unintended or wilful ignorance about the social context of the lives of distressed individuals and the therapeutic relationship itself could provoke an exasperated rejection of the legitimacy of psycho-therapy as being blinkered, futile, indulgent and individualistic. This is not my position but I can empathise with the impulse.

Indeed, much the same could be said of supervisors and super-vision. Not many writings on supervision stress the contextual issues that impact on the work with clients on one hand and on the work with supervisees as counsellors on the other hand. There is increasing awareness of the individual factors that must be considered, for example disability, race, sexual orientation. There is less awareness and articulation of the social contexts influencing therapeutic work. There is even less attention to the interaction of specific factors of the individual in conjunction with specific types of organizational culture (for example, gay men in an educational institution affiliated with a religious order that understands homosexuality as an unnatural or sinful way of life). Trained as counsellors and then supervisors many of us have used only an individually oriented perspective for solving problems, rather than considering the specific organizational factors that might strongly influence the professional's behaviour in context. Perhaps part of the reason for this is our own ignorance in understanding that impact: we are still novices in awareness of how organizational culture determines, or at least strongly influences, behaviour.

This book examines both critical individual factors and the organizational contexts in which supervision takes place. It lays out the cultural and systemic issues that arise in supervision from these individual and organizational characteristics. This view is in keeping with the times: there is a sense in which many professions are becoming more cognizant of 'systemic' perspectives. For example Keen (1994: xxi) writes:

> Systems theory has emerged as the dominant trend in most disciplines, from psychology to computer science, replacing the old method of piecemeal analysis, in which we broke everything down into its component parts. The tendency in recent thought is to stress synthesis, networks, interaction, process. The old notion that the whole is the sum of the parts has been replaced by the idea that the parts can only be understood as functions of the dynamics of the whole.

This book is divided into two parts. Part I deals with individual factors such as race, gender, disability and sexual orientation as crucial factors in supervision. Part II focuses on the contexts themselves in which counselling and, by association, supervision takes place: the educational, religious, industrial, medical and uniformed settings. We have asked practitioners who work in these settings and with these individual factors to speak from their experience. Our hope is that this book will contribute to the ever-growing literature on supervision and emphasize an often overlooked dimension – the context.

References

Alonso, A. (1985) *The Quiet Profession*. New York: Macmillan.

Hawkins, P. and Shohet, R. (1989) *Supervision in the Helping Professions*. Milton Keynes: Open University Press.

Keen, S. (1994) *Hymns to an Unknown God*. London: Piatkus.

Pilgrim, D. (1997) *Psychotherapy and Society*. London: Sage.

Smail, D. (1985) *Taking Care: An Alternative to Psychotherapy*. London: Dent and Sons.

I Supervision and client characteristics

1 Supervision and racial issues

Patricia Grant

Counselling supervision is a formal relationship in which a trainee or qualified counsellor presents his or her client work as a way of learning how to work more effectively with clients. This arrangement provides an opportunity for clients to get the best help possible, as well as aiding the professional development of the counsellor. This view has taken into consideration the BAC code of ethics, which stresses protection of the client when it states that: 'The primary purpose of supervision is to ensure the counsellor is addressing the needs of the client' (BAC 1988: B.1.1.). The first definition, however, goes a bit further by highlighting the importance of counsellor development. I think both are equally important because the more knowledge/skills counsellors have, the more likely they are to meet the needs of their client group. It is impossible to address adequately the needs of the client group if one is ignorant of that group's identity. Cook (1994) reminded us that race can be a prominent part of the identity of those who continually experience racial oppression, mainly because they are constantly reminded of their marginal status. It is therefore a mistake to view people solely on the basis of their universal identity, as that only leads to a loss of their individuality. Individuality plays a big part in counselling and supervision and most counsellors attend to it. Less attention, however, is paid to group identity. What is important in counselling and supervision is an integration of all three – individual, universal and group identity (Larson 1982). It is supervisors' responsibility to ensure that this integration takes place in supervision, and they achieve this by modelling during supervision as well as monitoring their supervisees' work with clients.

In this chapter the concept of race, in the context of supervision, will be explored. There will be a discussion of the need for supervisors to consider racial issues and to recognize specific racial dilemmas emerging in supervision. Finally, suggestions will be made on how supervisors can best be prepared to work with racial issues in supervision.

The concept of race

Christensen (1989: 275) defined race as 'an arbitrary classification of populations conceived in Europe, using actual or assumed genetic traits to classify populations of the world into a hierarchical order, with Europeans superior to all others'. One might question the value of the definition, particularly as it relates to genetics and its implication that one group is superior to others. People, however, are still judged on the basis of their skin colour so, whether one likes it or not, race is still relevant. Carter and Qureshi (1995: 251) wrote that 'Race is relevant because it is visible.' It is a basis for differentiating people – Black, White, Asian, etc. There are many races, but for the purpose of this chapter I will use two groupings – White and (to borrow a term from the USA) People of Colour. I have chosen the term 'People of Colour' because it is inclusive of non-White groups such as Blacks, Asian and Chinese, and as such is a useful grouping. It should be remembered, however, that many Black people in Britain do not like the term, because it brings to mind words such as 'Coloured' which has many negative connotations. There is certainly a need for a more accepted term to cover those races who are judged negatively on the basis of their skin colour.

Supervisors, counsellors and clients are all part of society and carry attitudes towards other races present within it – attitudes such as superiority, inferiority, resentment and fear. On approaching the counselling/supervisory situation, the players bring with them these attitudes which can then influence the working alliance; 'the history and the experience of the culturally different have been those of oppression, discrimination and racism' (Sue and Sue 1990: 78) and often this is the experience they will take with them to the counselling/supervisory relationship. The history of White people, on the other hand, is that of superiority over People of Colour and this is something they can take to the relationship which might influence it negatively. It is true to say that both People of Colour and White people tend to approach cross-racial relationships with caution. White people are cautious because they fear being seen as racist, and People of Colour are cautious as a way of protecting themselves from hurt. What then happens in situations such as these is that people sometimes say what they think others want them to say, rather than what they really feel and think. What we see here, then, is that race is a very important factor in any interaction across race, and whether it is addressed explicitly or not within cross-racial supervision, it will be there.

The effect of race on supervision

Supervision involves at least three people: the supervisor, the supervisee and the client. Although the client may not be physically present in the supervision room, he/she is often the focus of the supervision process. It is therefore important to consider the race of the client even if the supervisor and the supervisee are of the same race. Indeed, it might be even more important to do so in these circumstances as the chance of collusion is greater in such situations. Racial issues might surface in the supervision even when they are not being addressed in the counselling relationship. For example, a White counsellor working with a Black client might take to supervision problems of defensiveness on the part of the client and questioning the credibility and lack of openness of the client. This counsellor might not have considered that these problems could be related to racial factors and that past experience of racism and prejudice might make it difficult for the client to trust the counsellor (Sue and Sue 1990). As far as the counsellor is concerned, he/she is trustworthy and quite credible as a counsellor, and hence the problem is located in the client. Unfortunately, the situation is more complex and unless the topic of race is discussed openly there will be little opportunity to work through what might be at the heart of the distrust. I agree with Bernard and Goodyear (1992: 222) who write that 'most minority issues can be diffused with time when openness is encouraged'.

The goals, expectations and process of counselling might also be affected by the race of the parties involved. Brown and Landrum-Brown (1995) remind us that racial dynamics, the supervisor's frame of reference and his/her worldview will influence the content, process and outcome of supervision. Not only will supervision be influenced, but the type of counselling the client receives will be affected. It is therefore vital that these matters are addressed within supervision.

Negative perception of racial groups and how that could influence supervision

Blocks in supervision can occur because of racial differences between supervisor and supervisee. The blocks might include personal inhibitions on both sides. Cook and Helms (1988: 268) cite a study by Vander Kolk (1974) which suggested that 'prior to any supervision Black supervisees anticipated less supervisor empathy, respect and congruence than white supervisees'. If we accept this view then it is easy to see how these expectations might inhibit Black Supervisees' performance in supervision. Similarly, supervisors bring with them their own baggage and Cook and Helms (1988) cite Helms' (1982) unpublished thesis which indicated that a sample of predominantly White supervisors perceived Black, Asian and Hispanic supervisees, as being less able to accept constructive criticism and less open to self-examination. If this is the supervisors' perception of things it will certainly influence how they interpret the reality of the supervision situation and this could help to create a barrier that will not make for openness in supervision.

Supervisors might be critical of supervisees' interventions because they are different from the sort of interventions they themselves would use. This can pose a problem in supervision, particularly when the supervisor is of a different race from the supervisee and client. It might be that the supervisee is using an approach that is quite relevant to the client and how that racial group works; the supervisor, however, might be unfamiliar with the racial group and their behaviour. Below is an example of a situation that could cause possible conflict in supervision if the supervisor was unfamiliar with the context and the racial group.

Case study I

Anna is a counsellor who attends a large church whose members are predominantly Black. The church provides a counselling service for its members and they have employed as their counsellor Anna who is one of their own members. One of Anna's clients is Blossom whom she has been seeing for about three months. Blossom arrived at church one Sunday and was visibly upset. She wanted to see Anna immediately for counselling. Anna saw her, but instead of offering counselling she offered to get another church sister so they could pray for Blossom. It was a church meeting, and at church meetings Anna saw her role as church member *not* as counsellor; if a member wanted counselling then that could be offered in the counselling rooms on the agreed days and times. This was a boundary Anna had agreed with her clients in the church and it was one that she was called on here to reinforce.

The above situation might raise alarm bells for many supervisors and give rise to the following questions:

1   Should Anna be counselling people she meets in another social context?
2   Is it Anna's role to be praying for her clients?

To appreciate the situation one needs to understand that many of the Black people in this church could not afford to pay for counselling and would be denied such a service if the church did not provide it. Second, those who could afford it might not want to be counselled by someone who did not understand their context. A situation such as the one identified has many potential problems, and an easy way around it would be to avoid it – to say that counsellors should not work with people they know socially. This is a rather short-sighted view and one which does not take into consideration the needs of this group. It would be more helpful for the supervisor to help the supervisee look at how to work with the client group and safeguard their interests as well as those of the supervisee. One way of doing this would be to ensure that adequate boundaries are set up and maintained. In the above case study I was impressed with the counsellor's respect for the boundaries and the way she offered care while doing this.

Preparation of supervisors to work with racial issues

There are many examples of racial dynamics in supervision. For instance, how does the supervisee share feelings about racism experienced at work if he/she is uncertain about the supervisor's position on such matters? How does a supervisor of Colour work with a White supervisee who did not actively choose to be in supervision with that person. This sort of question needs to be addressed by all supervisors, and a starting point for this is through training. Bernard (1994: 67) points out the need for supervisor training in this area: 'the profession can no longer afford to accept as supervisors persons who are untrained in supervision or who have remained immune to multicultural issues within therapy and supervision'.

Cultural knowledge

We will now examine how supervisors might prepare themselves in order to manage the racial issues that could emerge in supervision. They need to be open-minded towards diversity and have knowledge and understanding of the racial groups they wish to work with. Often the frustration and anxiety in therapy is due to lack of understanding (Ibrahim 1985). I think the same can be said of supervision too. While it is impossible to learn about all the racial groups in society, it is only respectful to find out about those one works with on a consistent basis. Knowledge can be gained through reading, which will include literature, and material to do with the socio-political and historical context of the group. Art forms and plays are also a good source of information, along with discussion with people from these groups. Supervisees can also provide information, but they should never be seen as the main source of information. There is no excuse for supervisors failing to do their homework and then putting pressure, directly or indirectly, on supervisees to provide information that they, the supervisors, should have gathered elsewhere.

Cultural self-awareness

Supervisors also need to have a knowledge of their own racial group before they can begin to understand others and the impact race has on the lives of many people. I am amazed at the number of White therapist/supervisors in England who lack understanding of their own racial group. To a certain extent this is understandable because they are often not faced with the constant reminder that they are different; indeed it is others who are perceived as different. I would like to see supervisors everywhere asking themselves the following questions:

- Who am I racially?
- What is the history of my racial group?

- How does being a member of my racial group influence how I relate to others not in my group?
- What, if anything, would I like to change about how I relate to others who are not of my racial group?

If supervisors were to answer these kinds of questions and others of this nature they would then be in a better position to help their supervisees address them. The end result, I think, would be a more sensitive approach to counselling.

Attitude change

Knowledge about a group does not necessarily change attitudes. It is not unusual to rearrange or reinterpret new information so that we need not change our attitudes. For example we might have an attitude of superiority over another racial group and think that people belonging to that group are lacking in intelligence. On learning about highly intelligent people from that group we do not change our attitude but instead regard those intelligent people as different. Thus the supervisor, in addition to having knowledge, will also need to address his/her behaviour. One aspect of behaviour worth considering is the contact made with people of a different race. Discussing the sort of contact that is desirable, Ponterotto and Pedersen (1993: 92) write that it should be more than superficial if it is to allow the various parties to 'disconfirm stereotypes' about the respective groups. In countries such as Britain where there is a multi-racial population, most supervisors will know someone from another race. However, such knowledge might be limited. Some questions to help counsellors/supervisors identify the nature of their relationship with a person of another race are listed below.

- Identify ten people you know fairly well and who are of a different race from yourself.
- What is the nature of your relationship with each of the persons identified?
- Have you ever been invited to any of these people's homes? If yes, what was the occasion of the visit?
- Have you invited any of these people to your home? If yes, what was the occasion of the visit?
- What do you know of these peoples' experience of living in a predominantly White society? How did you gain this information?

- Have you ever had a discussion with these people on the topic of race? If yes, how did the discussion get started and how did it end? How did you feel about having such a discussion?
- What do you know of the support systems of these people?
- How comfortable do you feel with the differences that exist between you and the racially different people you have identified? How does this level of comfort/discomfort manifest itself?
- Are you aware of any stereotypical views you hold of any of the racial groups you are in contact with? If yes, how do these views influence how you relate to these people?

Using the initial meeting between supervisor/supervisee to address racial issues

The initial meeting between the supervisor and the supervisee provides many opportunities for the subject of race to be addressed. For example, in exploring the supervisee's experience of supervision, the supervisor can find out the race, gender, etc., of past supervisors and see how the supervisee worked with those people. It is important to obtain this information quite early because the supervisee's past experience of supervision will influence how they function in supervision in the present.

Case study 2

Janet is a Black woman who has been working part-time as a counsellor for a number of years. For the last two years she has been in supervision with a Black supervisor to whom she relates very well. She has now been offered a full-time counselling post but her new employer, who is White, wants her to be supervised by an accredited supervisor, and her present supervisor is not accredited. Janet is given the opportunity to choose her own supervisor with the proviso that the supervisor meets this condition. Janet is somewhat resentful about having to make the change because she feels her present supervisor understands her needs and the needs of her clients who are mainly Black. She also feels that she does not really have much of a choice, since it would be difficult to find a Black supervisor who was accredited and hence she would have to choose someone White.

Questions

1   Assuming that you are: (a) a White supervisor
                          (b) a Black supervisor
    How might Janet's history/past experience of supervision
    influence how she engages with you in supervision?
2   What are some of the things you might do as a supervisor
    to facilitate your engagement with Janet?

*(Possible answers to these questions are given at the end of the
chapter.)*

In exploring supervisees' experiences supervisors will also ascertain the sorts of clients they work with. It is often fairly easy to find out the ethnic origins of clients when one is discussing the supervisee's case load. It is also useful at this point to find out the sort of experience and training the supervisees have had in working with the clients they have identified. This type of information will give supervisors some insight into the sort of monitoring they will need to do and an idea of the knowledge and skills they will need to supervise the counsellor. Basically, the sorts of questions that the supervisor will need to ask when dealing with counsellors working with multi-racial groups are:

*   What do I know about racial identity development models? What does my supervisee know of them?
*   What skills does my supervisee have for working with clients at different stages of their identity development?
*   How will I monitor his/her work with clients of a different race?
*   How comfortable do I feel about supervising someone whose case load is made up of clients who are of a different race to mine? How might I monitor that my skills are up to the job?

Learning needs of different racial groups

A large component of supervision is about education; hence it is important for supervisors to ascertain how best their supervisees learn. This needs to be done quite early in the supervision, preferably in the assessment stage. Unless supervisees' learning needs are met, then supervision will not be effective. Regardless of the race of the individual, learning styles will differ from supervisee to supervisee and this will in turn influence how they present material for supervision and how much they absorb from supervision. Often supervisors will supervise in the way they like to be supervised, rather than focus on the needs of the supervisee, so, for example, a supervisor might expect a lot of written material from their supervisees. This might not go down well with supervisees who are from an oral culture and who prefer to talk rather than write. There are also supervisees who might learn more from active teaching in supervision rather than being recommended to read an article. An active teaching approach might be more in keeping with a culture in which stories are passed down by word of mouth rather than by children reading story books. Similarly, active learning styles such as the use of role-playing in supervision might be more acceptable to some racial groups than others who would go for a more passive style. It is therefore vital that the supervisor finds out which style is best suited to their supervisees.

The supervisory relationship

The supervisory relationship starts from the time the supervisee makes the initial contact with the supervisor. The quality and effectiveness of the supervisory relationship is vital if supervision is to meet the needs of those concerned. If the supervisor and supervisee are from different races, this should be acknowledged quite soon in the relationship. Inskipp and Proctor (1989) highlight the need to establish a supervision contract as a means of ensuring a productive supervisory relationship. In negotiating this contract the supervisor and supervisee should discuss how they feel about working with each other. This is important for any supervisory relationship, but where the relationship is cross-racial, it becomes even more important. The major task of the supervisor at this stage is to build trust and openness and self-disclosure as a means of facilitating this. Bradley (1989: 36) reported that negative supervision was characterized by 'mistrust, disrespect and lack of honest self-disclosure'. Agreement on how the relationship will be monitored is also useful in ensuring a satisfactory relationship.

There are certain fears and anxieties that might influence the supervisory relationship, for example 'dominance anxiety' (Rioch 1980). This term refers to a power–authority dimension where supervisors are seen as all-powerful. This can be seen in any sort of supervision but it takes on an added significance when the supervisor is White and the supervisee is a Person of Colour, as the supervisor's dominant position within the supervision can stir up feelings about White dominance. Performance anxiety might also occur at the start of the relationship; here the supervisee is keen on getting the approval of the supervisor and sees perfection as a way of achieving it. Again this is not peculiar to cross-racial supervision but it can be a salient factor in situations where the supervisor is White and the supervisee is a Person of Colour. Many People of Colour, in Britain for example, have learned that to get ahead they have to do 'better' than their White colleagues. This can mean a constant striving for perfection and a fear of showing work that might not be judged 'perfect'. In addition, there are White supervisors who hold stereotypical views regarding People of Colour, and this might lead to patronizing approaches in supervision resulting in supervisees feeling deskilled or wanting and supervisors taking on the 'expert' role.

The responsibility of the supervisor

Much of the focus in this chapter has been on supervisors and what they need to do. This has been deliberate, because in most cases it is supervisors who have the power and are in a position to ensure that racial matters are attended to in supervision. Take the situation where a White supervisor is allocated to a supervisee of Colour who perceives the supervisor as someone with little understanding of her world. It is unlikely that the supervisee will raise the issue of race, fearing a bad report or reference; hence it might be easier to keep a low profile and say very little. Alternatively, a White supervisee who is allocated to a supervisor of Colour might find it difficult to discuss negative feelings about clients who are Black for fear of being seen as racist. Supervisors must therefore take the responsibility for raising the issue of making it safe to discuss these matters. This does not exempt supervisees from their responsibilities in supervision and some questions that supervisees might ask themselves as a way of preparing for supervision are given below.

The responsibility of the supervisee

Before meeting the supervisor, supervisees might like to ask themselves the following questions:

- What sort of supervisor do I require? Does it matter if this person is the same race as myself or not?
- What inhibitions do I have with regards to working with a supervisor of another race? How might these inhibitions get in the way of supervision? What could I do to ensure it did not happen?
- What qualities do I expect my supervisor to have? How will I go about assessing if they are there?
- How will I go about discovering whether or not my supervisor has an understanding of my client's and my worldview?
- How will I share my own views about race and its place in supervision with this supervisor?
- At what stage of development am I in terms of my own racial identity? How will being at this stage influence my approach to supervision? (See the model of Atkinson in Sue and Sue (1990) and Helms' model (1995) for more information about racial identity frameworks.)

During the assessment interview with a Supervisor, supervisees might like to consider the following points:

- Remember that assessment is a two-way process and that you are assessing the supervisor at the same time as you are being assessed. You will need to check out the supervisor's experience in dealing with differences, and in this case racial difference.
- Be open to diversity and assess your supervisor's level of openness.
- Pay attention to your feelings, own them and express them in ways that are respectful to yourself and the other party.
- Ask the supervisor for what you want – you will stand a better chance of getting it if you do.
- Agree with the supervisor how you will monitor your relationship.

In ongoing supervision, the following might be worth doing:

- Bring to supervision situations where race is a relevant feature but keep in mind that not all of your clients' problems revolve around the topic of race.
- Go into each meeting with your supervisor trusting him/her to do well by you and your client. Adopt this approach unless there is reason for you not to.

Note: Supervisees of Colour should not allow themselves to be set up as experts on all matters pertaining to People of Colour. This is an impossible task and it is not what they are in supervision to do.

Cross-racial issues that might emerge in supervision

Supervisors will find below a case study that will help them to explore further some of the cross-racial issues that might occur in supervision.

Case study 3

Jasmine is a mixed-race British woman with an Asian mother and a Black father. Jasmine does not mix socially with People of Colour, and the people she calls friends are all White. There are some Black people where she is now working and ever since she started there they have been inviting her to a Black awareness group. Reluctantly she attended one of these meetings and while she was there she commented that she had White friends and 'they don't mind her'. This statement drew a lot of anger from the rest of the group as they demanded 'Why should they mind you?' 'What do you mean they don't mind you?' Jasmine, in turn, got angry with the group but she was also angry with herself as, in seeking to answer their question, she became aware of her position in the awareness group and how hard she worked to be accepted by her White friends. On leaving the meeting Jasmine felt upset. She did not like herself very much and a couple of weeks later decided to see a counsellor. The counsellor she chose to see (Pam) was White.

Imagine you are Pam's supervisor and Pam has brought this client to supervision. Ask yourself the following questions:

- Why do you think Jasmine chose Pam as her counsellor?
- Where would you say the client was in terms of her ethnic identity development? (If you are unfamiliar with ethnic identity models see Sue and Sue (1990) for that of Atkinson and others, or Ponterotto et al. (1995) for that of Helms.)
- How would you help the counsellor to work with Jasmine at that identity stage?
- What are the advantages and disadvantages for Jasmine in working with a White counsellor?

- What are the advantages and disadvantages for Jasmine in working with a counsellor of similar ethnic origins to herself?
- What other issues would you need to address?

Conclusion

Race is visible, and while one does not want to over-emphasize difference of race, it would be a mistake to ignore it. A person's race is a very important part of who he or she is, and therefore must receive acknowledgement. It is the supervisor's job to ensure that issues of race are addressed when working cross-racially. Supervisors also have a responsibility for obtaining the necessary information about racial groups in their catchment area, if they plan on working with those groups of people. Supervisors are part of society and possess many of the prejudices that can be seen in it. They therefore need to be open to self-examination if they are to work effectively with other races apart from their own. Finally, let us remember that the hardest part of dealing with racial issues in supervision is at the start of the relationship. If the matter is brought out openly and discussed honestly, then it is likely that a trusting relationship will develop and supervison will be fruitful.

Possible answers to questions raised in case study 2

1 (a) Anger at White employer might be projected on to White supervisor.
         She might distrust White people who put obstacles in her way and reduce her choice, for example her employer.
         She might fear not being understood. She was understood by her Black supervisor but now is unsure whether a White supervisor will be able to understand.
         She might use her past supervisor as an ideal for the new one to match up to and so the new supervisor is constantly being judged.
1 (b) On the surface it would seem that engagement with a Black supervisor would be easy, but this might not be the case. The supervisee could have greater expectations of this person as being like the previous supervisor, and if

the new supervisor does not live up to this image, then he or she is no good.

2   The supervisor might find that in providing the following, he/she can facilitate engagement with Janet:

- the opportunity to discuss her past experience and to share what she got from her past supervisor and what she would want from the present relationship;
- respect for what Janet had with the other supervisor and an acknowledgement of the importance of that relationship to Janet;
- an openness and willingness to make appropriate self-disclosures, for example disclosure related to how the supervisor feels about her present interaction with Janet;
- coming across as genuine and sincere and not just putting on a show for the supervisee's benefit.

References

BAC (British Association for Counselling) (1988) *Code of Ethics and Practice for the Supervision of Counsellors*. Rugby: BAC.

Bernard, J. (1994) 'Multicultural supervision: a reaction to Leong and Wagner, Cook, Priest and Fukuyama', *Counselor Education and Supervision*, 34: 159–71.

Bernard, J. and Goodyear, R. (1992) *Fundamentals of Clinical Supervision*. Boston, MA: Allyn & Bacon.

Bradley, L. (1989) *Counselor Supervision*. Manic, IN: Accelerated Development Inc.

Brown, M. and Landrum-Brown, J. (1995) 'Counselor supervision: cross-cultural perspectives', in J. Ponterotto, J. Casas, L. Suzuki and C. Alexander (eds) *Handbook of Multicultural Counseling*. Thousand Oaks, CA: Sage.

Carter, R. and Qureshi, A. (1995) 'A typology of philosophical assumptions in multicultural counseling and training', in J. Ponterotto, J. Casas, L. Suzuki and C. Alexander (eds) *Handbook of Multicultural Counseling*. Thousand Oaks, CA: Sage.

Christensen, C. (1989) 'Cross-cultural awareness development: a conceptual model', *Counselor Education and Supervision*, 28: 270–87.

Cook, D. (1994) 'Racial identity in supervision', *Counselor Education and Supervision*, 34 (December): 132–41.

Cook, D. and Helms, J. (1988) 'Visible racial/ethnic group supervisees' satisfaction with cross-cultural supervision as predicted by relationship characteristics', *Journal of Counseling Psychology*, 35: 268–73.

Helms, J. (1982) *Differential evaluation of minority and majority counseling trainees practicum preference*. University of Maryland: unpublished thesis.

Helms, J. (1995) 'An update of Helms' white and people of color racial identity model', in J. Ponterotto, J. Casas, L. Suzuki and C. Alexander (eds) *Handbook of Multicultural Counseling*. Thousand Oaks, CA: Sage.

Ibrahim, F. (1985) 'Effective cross-cultural counseling and psychotherapy: a framework', *The Counseling Psychologist*, 13 (October): 625–36.

Inskipp, F. and Proctor, B. (1989) *Skills for Supervising and Being Supervised* (Principles of Counselling Audiotape Series). East Sussex: Alexia.

Larson, P.C. (1982) 'Counseling Special Populations', *Professional Psychology*, 13 (6): 843–58.

Ponterotto, J. and Pedersen, P. (1993) *Preventing Prejudice*. London: Sage.

Ponterotto, J., Casas, J., Suzuki, L. and Alexander, C. (eds) (1995) *Handbook of Multicultural Counselling*. Thousand Oaks, CA: Sage.

Rioch, M. (1980) 'The dilemmas of supervision in dynamic psychotherapy', in A. Hess (ed.) *Psychotherapy Supervision: Theory, Research and Practice*. New York: John Wiley, pp. 68–76.

Sue, D. and Sue, D. (1990) *Counseling the Culturally Different*. New York: John Wiley.

Vander Kolk, C.J. (1974) 'The relationship of personality, values and race to anticipation of the supervisory relationship', *Rehabilitation Counseling Bulletin*, 18 (1): 41–6.

2 Supervision and gender issues

Mary Lee Nelson and Elizabeth Holloway

'Gender' is a rather asexual, neutral-sounding word that categorizes not only 'we animate beings', but reaches into language itself, rendering even sexless objects as feminine or masculine. Gender has played a hand in the grammatical structure of our language and our fate as men and women. Gender has decided who goes to war, who knits (apologies to the modernly motivated Kaffe Fassett), and who has the 'big jobs' (as the daughter of one of us once said). Gender has been used as a reason and explanation for human behaviour from colour preferences to aptitude at maths to controlling the television remote control. Men and women are clearly biologically different and therefore play different reproductive roles. However, around this fundamental difference, there has been created a whole literature of power and politics, and men and women. In the workplace, talk about 'gender' and between 'genders' is a subject of some anxiety, confusion, frustration, humiliation, amusement and triumph. In professional hierarchical relationships policies and laws have been codified to ensure the protection of the vulnerable party (the person who controls less formal power in the workplace), 'the underling', and prevent the abuse of power by the 'overling'. Supervision of counsellors-in-training where the supervisee will be formally evaluated constitutes a hierarchical relationship with formalized roles and professional objectives. The contract between supervisor and supervisee might explicitly state expectations for process, learning goals of the supervisee, structure of meetings, and other important clarifications. However, it is in the implicit world of assumptions, perceptions, judgements and social expectations that the insidious politics of cross-gender behaviours emerge. It is in the talk of supervision that the nuances of gender are manifested.

We begin this chapter with snippets of discourse from two cross-gender supervisory relationships: a female supervisor with a male supervisee and a male supervisor with a female supervisee. The supervision takes place in a counsellor-training context, that is, supervisors are doctoral students in counselling providing supervision for masters students in counselling. No instructions had been given to the participants regarding what to discuss and all the supervision sessions were audiotaped to avoid idiosyncratic effects of taping only for these purposes. We have chosen these excerpts because gender issues appear with some degree of subtlety. Each scenario illustrates the kind of tension that can take place within a cross-sex supervisor–supervisee dyad.

In the first scenario, the concern involves the client's gender and what kind of intervention might be appropriate for the client. In the second scenario, the concern involves trainee concerns about gender in the supervisor–trainee relationship. Conflict in supervision that is based on gender can play out at either or both of these levels. We will first present a scenario, then discuss the gender issues that emerged and how these situations might be managed in supervision.

Scenario 1: Female supervisor with a male trainee

Supervisor: It really helps to just really break through for somebody just to name the feelings. And I think it is because [the person] feels, 'I'm being heard.'

Trainee: OK. Well, we'll see if it works on guys too, huh?

Supervisor: Yeah.

Trainee: 'Cuz I haven't found many that can get in touch.

Supervisor: [*playing a videotape*] See how angry he is?

Trainee: I think I'm taking it too cognitively, the things that are going through my head. I'm not making process statements. Because I knew he was angry from his voice and his delivery.

Supervisor: Well, he hasn't gotten away from his emotions yet.

Trainee: But I think you're right. What I could have done is make a process statement.

Discussion of Scenario 1

In Scenario 1, the female supervisor is attempting to get her male supervisee to recognize the client's anger as shown in the videotape of the counselling interaction. She was urging the supervisee to acknowledge the client's feeling. Notice how she softens the directness of her suggestion by using the qualifier 'I think it is because . . .' and proceeds to suggest that such an affirmation for the client would increase the sense of 'being heard'. Essentially she is directing the supervisee to reflect the feeling and consequently increase empathy. Certainly reflecting feelings is not a particularly controversial skill in counselling in that most theoretical and empirical orientations would identify empathy as a necessary therapeutic condition. However, the supervisee responds, 'We'll see if it works on guys too, huh?' (tonality forceful and questioning), as if the client, 'being a guy', might render such an intervention ineffective. We would hypothesize that the supervisee was feeling challenged on three counts. First, as a member of the male group his proprietary interests and knowledge of what men need was being called into question by a female, a non-group member. Second, the supervisor holds formal legitimate power in this context, that is, evaluating and providing feedback on the supervisee's skills. The supervisee responds by claiming power to knowledge through the privilege of his gender, thus subtly undermining the legitimate authority of the supervisor. Third, the supervisee, experiencing anxiety about being required to manage a feeling discussion with another male, was protecting his own vulnerability and discomfort with feelings.

The concern of the male supervisee that perhaps a male client may have difficulty getting in touch with emotion, represents an issue that is central to the struggle of contemporary males in western cultures and to male citizens of cultures that come into contact with western values. Restrictive emotionality is a primary characteristic of gender role strain (Pleck 1981) or gender role conflict (O'Neill 1981), a psychologically anxious state related to culturally determined male role expectations that conflict with the interpersonal demands of marriage, family or work environment (O'Neill, Good and Holmes 1995). Restrictive emotionality has been found to predict men's dissatisfaction with marriage and family relationships (Campbell and Snow 1992) and health risks related to anger and anxiety (Eisler, Skidmore and Ward 1988). Levant (1995, 1996) and Pollack (1995) emphasize the intense dilemma many men face between wanting intimacy on one hand and fearing the exposure and vulnerability intimate contact brings. Both authors point out the powerful injunction that gender role socialization places upon boys to limit feelings and become stoic in the face of adversity. The counselling process emphasizes intimacy, and expression of affect can be threatening to men in a way that women counsellors and supervisors may have difficulty comprehending. Socialization commonly does not prepare young males to engage in discussions about relationships and feelings (Fivush 1989; Levant 1995), and many men may feel incompetent in such an arena. Men have been socialized to express their vulnerability or incompetence by being angry or aggressive and effectively defending against the threat of closeness or vulnerability. Still the emotional arousal is being discharged through the direct expression of anger or more indirectly warding off the attack by discounting the relevancy of the perceived criticism.

Sells, Goodyear, Lichtenberg and Polkinghorne (1997) invest-igated focus in supervision discourse for cross- and same-gender dyads and found that of several possible relationship foci, the male–male supervision dyads preferred to focus on the client significantly more often than any other dyad type. They empha-size that the male–male dyads preferred to discuss client cases rather than to address either the counselling or the supervisory relationship. This finding implies that men in clinical relationships may experience discomfort with discussion of relationships – at least with other men, thus resulting in their avoidance of close affiliation. Clinical situations may threaten men in two ways: they require the identification and expression of feelings, and they may require a man to engage in a process that makes him feel incompe-tent, a move that may result in concomitant feelings of power-lessness.

The woman supervisor in Scenario 1, who emphasized that her male supervisee should attend more to his male client's affect, did not engage her supervisee in a discussion of men's issues related to the relational–affective domain. She did not argue her point after the supervisee's challenge that her suggestion would likely not work with men. Rather, she turned to the evidence, that is, the videotape, and pointed out the client's implicit expression of feeling. This effectively took it back to the client and moved it from a power struggle between supervisor and supervisee based on gender-privilege. After watching the tape, the supervisee seems more willing to examine his skills and comes up with his own analysis of the need to make process statements in light of the client's anger. Upon his acceptance of the presence of the client's feelings, the supervisor then suggests that it wasn't that bad after all because the client still remained with his feelings. With this reinforcement the supervisee ostensibly agrees with the supervisor and reframes the suggestion to deal with feelings to the more neutral 'make a process statement'. Although the supervisor was partially successful in having the supervisee reconsider his intervention and suggest a reasonable alternative, she did not deal with his feelings of being vulnerable in the face of emotional talk between men – thus missing an opportunity to discuss that he, as well as his client, may have been struggling with his feelings. Working with male clients and supervisees requires both awareness of how vulnerable men may feel in a session with a powerful other (whether male or female) and patience with regard to their level of readiness to express and address affect. A supervisee's reluctance to do so with a male client, particularly in the early phases of counselling, may be based upon an accurate assessment of the client's developmental needs in the clinical situation. A male colleague of Mary Lee Nelson, who specializes in working with men, recommends asking a male client how it feels to 'let down' with a male counsellor after the first few sessions. He cautions against using the word 'vulnerable', which is more difficult for men to tolerate, but he emphasizes how important it is to address the unusual arrangement between men in intimate relationships that emphasizes one's difficulties rather than triumphs.

Because the goals of counselling and of supervision both involve understanding the affective/relational domain, it is important to address how gender role conflict may inhibit the discussion of supervisee feelings as they occur in counselling and supervision. It is probable that the female supervisor in Scenario 1 was not cognizant of the type of anxiety a male supervisee may feel in counselling with a male client, although she effectively subverted a power struggle based on gender and instead used her role as supervisor to return to the task of viewing the counselling interaction.

Scenario 2: Male supervisor with a female trainee

Supervisor: Let's talk about how you're feeling right now.
Trainee: OK. Um . . . I'm . . . I'm.
Supervisor: I'm feeling maybe something may be going on.
Trainee: Well, it's . . . I think what I'm gonna . . . I'm gonna just have to work on this. I do . . . I just don't even know if I can articulate it very well. I think I need to work at taking criticism better than I do.
Supervisor: Do you feel like I've been criticizing you?

Trainee: A little bit. Um . . . I guess.

Supervisor: It's OK.

Trainee: It just feels really silly. Well, it might not, but it does.

Supervisor: Mm hm. OK.

Trainee: I think that . . . I was sitting here feeling like . . . I don't know . . . It's funny . . . I was thinking a few minutes ago it would have been better if I had had a woman as my supervisor. But I think . . . 'cause . . . I think I do well . . . and sometimes, like, I don't really know why.

Supervisor: Can you help me understand this, what's happening right now?

Trainee: I guess it taps into my feelings of insecurity and inadequacy and things like that. And I think they do tend to come out a lot more in situations with men than with women. So I don't know where that derives from, but I can sometimes feel like I should be able . . . I shouldn't be responding like this.

Supervisor: Well, you are responding like this.

Discussion of Scenario 2

In Scenario 2, the male supervisor is surprised by his female supervisee's admission that she feels uncomfortable working with males and her suggestion that she might have done better with a woman supervisor. Having confessed these feelings, she chides herself for harbouring such preferences. Her reaction is quite complex and requires scrutiny at more than one level. The first level is that of the supervisor–supervisee interaction. Prior to this discussion the supervisor had been attempting to get his supervisee, who was working with an adolescent boy, to tell him what she knew about adolescent boys. He had directly asked her, 'What do you know about adolescent boys?' Thus, not only had this supervisee brought into the relationship gender-based conflicts with male authority figures, but this male authority figure had introduced gender into the supervision and challenged her regarding her knowledge of boys. Contextually, she was surrounded by men and responds to this situation by confessing that she is inadequate and unfit because she cannot deal with criticism and more specifically with men who criticize her (that is, her supervisor). Unlike the male in our first scenario who challenged any suggestion of criticism, this female supervisee is 'overly' responsible for the interaction with her supervisor. She blames herself for not being able to take care of her feelings towards her supervisor, for having such feelings, and for not being able to articulate them coherently. However, she uses the gender defence, as the male supervisee did. Notice her comment that she would do better with a woman as her supervisor. Thus, she protects herself from the supervisor's implied criticism by disempowering his potential impact based on his gender. She departs company from the supervisee in Scenario 1 by then speaking fully about her underlying feelings regarding men. She protects the supervisor from any implied insult to his competence by blaming herself for having these feelings and further by naming them as a sign of incompetence.

This line of interpretation reflects our understanding that supervision relationships can be described in part around the embodiment and exercise of power. The power awarded the supervisor is related to the role, but the social construction of gender in relation to power is a substructure on which supervisory relationships are built. Gender has been found to relate to power in supervisory relationships in a number of ways. We found gender differences for men and women supervisees with regard to how much power they were accorded in supervision by their supervisors (Nelson and Holloway 1990). Both men and women supervisors provided more reinforcement for expressions of interpersonal power in the supervisory interaction with men supervisees than with women. Concomitantly, the women supervisees assumed less interpersonal power in the interactions than did the men. In a related investigation, Granello, Beamish and Davis (1997) found that both men and women supervisors requested supervisee opinions and conceptualizations significantly more often for men supervisees than for women, thus allowing the men the interpersonal power that comes from assuming the expert position. The results of these two studies suggest that supervisors might inadvertently grant less power in the relationship to their women supervisees than to men. These studies have implications with regard to attending to the gender of the supervisee. It may be that supervisors need to be aware that their women supervisees need more help than the men in assuming power in the interaction. This is a interesting paradox of 'having the power to empower another in a relationship of hierarchical structure', but one not uncommon to therapeutic contexts. Some modern feminists stress the importance of equality of power in therapeutic relationships. They underscore the significance of a counsellor's professional role as a powerful one and recommend using the therapeutic relationship to empower the client, downplaying the power of the counsellor (Brown and Brodsky 1992). Supervision might also be used as a vehicle for empowering women in a professional relationship. Nelson (1997) has recommended specific interpersonal techniques for empowering women in supervision.

Another finding of the Granello et al. study related to supervisor and supervisee behaviour over time. They found that only dyads with male supervisees predictably followed developmental theories that suggest supervision becomes more collegial over time, with the supervisor offering fewer interventions and the supervisee offering more (Hogan 1964; Littrell, Lee-Borden and Lorenz 1979; Stoltenberg and Delworth 1987). Dyads with women supervisees, however, over time appeared to reflect a greater imbalance of power. Women supervisees in relationships that had lasted more than a year offered fewer suggestions and opinions in session that those who had been in supervision for six months or less. Thus, female supervisees may tend to relinquish power over time, giving in to a form of social role conditioning (Eagly 1987) that requires women to be deferent. Certainly, we notice in Scenario 2 the confusion of the supervisee in 'blaming the supervisor' for her discomfort only through her own incompetence to handle criticism from a male (*ergo* him). It is unlikely that the supervisor in Scenario 2 was able to anticipate his supervisee's reaction to his challenging question regarding adolescent boys.

Perhaps a discussion of power in supervision is really incomplete without considering the interaction of affiliation, a dimension often closely related to power (Leary 1957). Judith Jordan (1991) addressed a woman's need for a sense of mutuality in primary relationships. She contended that a woman's sense of self-esteem depends in part upon her experience of relational competence, her capacity to establish healthy connections and participate with others in a mutual give-and-take of understanding and empathy. Cultural feminists emphasize interpersonal connection in their writings about the type of therapeutic relationship women require (Gilligan 1991; Greene 1990; Jack 1991; Jordan 1991; Nelson 1996). Women seem to respond more favourably when working with a woman therapist, a context of gender familiarity. Studies of female client populations have demonstrated higher satisfaction and outcome ratings for women clients who worked with women counsellors than for women clients who worked with men (Jones, Krupnick and Kerig 1987; Kirshner,

Genack and Hauser 1978). Thus, the very thing that makes women comfortable in intimate relationships might be the very thing that causes discomfort for men.

A male supervisor may need to overcome some of his discomfort with intimacy in order to create a safe relationship within which a female supervisee can grow and learn. We recommend using the affiliative domain to invite female supervisees to assume power (Holloway 1995; Nelson 1997). Female supervisees' mastery in conceptualization of the relational aspects of the case may offer opportunities for women to assume power in a domain where they feel an ease of expertise. However, just as the male supervisee needs to explore the 'emotional realm of therapeutic understanding', so too the female supervisee must go beyond her natural affiliative posture and be comfortable in directly confronting and challenging constructively in both the counselling and supervisory relationships. Scenario 2 provides an good example of a supervisory intervention that attempts to use affiliation to empower the supervisee. Recall that the supervisee, after confronting her supervisor with her discomfort in having a male supervisor, then recanted, 'I shouldn't be feeling like this.' The supervisor, rather than interpreting her feelings or defending himself, chose to validate her feelings ('Well, you are feeling like this'). His focus turned to the dynamic between them rather than on her as the source of the discomfort. He invited her to tell him when she felt uncomfortable with him, and assured her that he would be responsive. Thus, the supervisor used the affective/relational domain within which to approach his supervisee's anxiety about working with a man. He also acknowledged that his responses to her might not be perfect and invited her to correct him. This position on his part eventually led the pair to establish a collaborative, enthusiastic and respectful supervisory relationship. Though moving into the relational/affective domain with his supervisee was not easy for the male supervisor, both supervisor and supervisee benefited greatly from her taking the risk to challenge the relationship (albeit with misgivings) and from his reframing the conflict from her problem to their opportunity to understand.

Same-gender supervisory dyads

The two scenarios highlighted in this chapter illustrated cross-gender supervision interactions. Same-gender supervision dyads have their own inherent challenges and advantages. In their extensive review of studies that compared demographically matched to non-matched counselling dyads, Beutler and Clarkin (1990) found that the matched pairs were more successful. They suggested that clients paired with counsellors of similar demographic backgrounds seem to do better because the clients want the familiarity and empathy that such matches often offer. It is likely that some supervisees may experience similar safety with same-sex supervisors.

In the case of a women supervisee, the sense that a female supervisor has some experiences in common with her accomplishes two things: it enhances her feeling of connection with the supervisor, and it allows her to feel more power in the relationship than she might feel with a male supervisor. Thus, a woman supervisee might benefit from (a) a supportive sense of connection, and (b) an opportunity to examine her own reactions and use of personal power.

Similarly, a male counsellor with a male supervisor may experience the comfort that is derived from working with someone who understands his struggle working in the relational/affective domain. The male supervisor may be able to help the supervisee process his uncertainties and develop skills that allow him to feel more competent in the emotional domain. However, if the male supervisor is himself still uncomfortable with addressing relational/affective matters, the pair could collude to emphasize the cognitive/analytic level. Like the female supervisee, the male supervisee has two challenges: (a) he needs to experience understanding and acceptance that he may not be as certain about managing intimate relationships as well as feelings of mastery and adversity; and (b) he needs to feel empowered to expand his affiliative skills, including a willingness to appreciate the emotional domain as a resource for therapeutic understanding and intervention. Beutler and Clarkin (1990) contend that, regardless of demographics, what people really need in a clinical relationship is a sense that they share some attitudes and beliefs with their helpers. However, in our opinion the over-reliance on match in gender (or other demographic characteristics) may truncate the counsellor's development by inadvertently reinforcing their known ways of being in relationships and not stretching their awareness and skills to areas less familiar. Awareness gained by working through relationships across gender can be of great value in working within gender. Demographic match is less important than awareness of specific needs and style of interaction that supervisees might bring. Reading these needs and having the self-awareness and skills to flex supervisory interventions to facilitate learning is the more critical factor.

Concluding remarks

As supervisors, we must come to understand our own 'gendered world' as it has informed the social context in which have lived and now live. Our personal historical relationships have informed our understanding of being with the 'other gender' and these experiences are implicitly a part of the professional relationship of supervision. There are different phases of supervisees learning their profession in which they might have particular opportunities by being in a same- or cross-gendered pairing in supervision. The growing edges of their personal development as a man, or as a woman, and the relationships that have informed their understanding of this gendered world are intrinsically connected to their professional role and therapeutic work. All professional counsellors who plan to conduct supervision need to be aware of gender differences that can affect their work and work towards developing the necessary skills to address those differences as they may arise in the interpersonal context of the supervisory relationship.

References

Beutler, L.E. and Clarkin, J.F. (1990) *Systematic Treatment Selection: Toward Targeted Therapeutic Interventions.* New York: Bruner/Mazel.

Brown, L.S. and Brodsky, A.M. (1992) 'The future of feminist therapy', *Psychotherapy: Theory, Research, and Practice,* 29: 51–7.

Campbell, J.L. and Snow, B.M. (1992) 'Gender role conflict and family environment as predictors of men's marital satisfaction', *Journal of Family Psychology,* 6: 84–7.

Eagly, A.H. (1987) *Sex Differences in Social Behavior: A Social Role Interpretation.* Hillsdale, NJ: Erlbaum.

Eisler, R.M., Skidmore, J.R. and Ward, C.H. (1988) 'Masculine gender-role stress: predictor of anger, anxiety, and health-risk behaviors', *Journal of Personality Assessment,* 52: 133–41.

Fivush, R. (1989) 'Exploring sex differences in the emotional content of mother–child conversations about the past', *Sex Roles,* 20: 675–91.

Gilligan, C. (1991) 'Women's psychological development: implications for psycho-therapy', *Women in Therapy*, 11 (3–4): 5–31.

Granello, D.H., Beamish, P.M. and Davis, T.E. (1997) 'Supervisee empowerment: Does gender make a difference?', *Counselor Education and Supervision*, 36: 305–17.

Greene, G.D. (1990) 'Is separation really so great?' in L.S. Brown and M.F. Root (eds) *Diversity and Complexity in Feminist Therapy*. New York: Harrington Park Press, pp. 87–104.

Hogan, R.A. (1964) 'Issues and approaches in supervision', *Psychotherapy: Research and Practice*, 18: 209–16.

Holloway, E.L. (1995) *Clinical Supervision: A Systems Approach*. Thousand Oaks, CA: Sage.

Holloway, E.L., Freund, R.D., Gardner, S.L., Nelson, M.L. and Walker, B.R. (1989) 'Relation of power and involvement to theoretical orientation in supervision: an analysis of discourse', *Journal of Counseling Psychology*, 36: 88–102.

Jack, D.C. (1991) *Silencing the Self: Women and Depression*. Cambridge, MA: Harvard University Press.

Jones, E.E., Krupnick, J.L. and Kerig, P.K. (1987) 'Some gender effects in brief psychotherapy', *Psychotherapy*, 24: 336–52.

Jordan, J.V. (1991) 'Empathy, mutuality, and therapeutic change: clinical implications of a relational model', in J.V. Jordan, A.G. Kaplan, J.B. Miller, I.P. Stiver and J.L. Surrey (eds) *Women's Growth in Connection*. New York: Guilford Press, pp. 283–9.

Kirshner, L.A., Genack, A. and Hauser, S.T. (1978) 'Effects of gender on short-term psychotherapy', *Psychotherapy: Theory, Research, and Practice*, 15: 158–67.

Leary, T. (1957) *Interpersonal Diagnosis of Personality*. New York: Ronald Press.

Levant, R.F. (1995) 'Toward the reconstruction of masculinity', in R.F. Levant and W.S. Pollack (eds) *A New Psychology of Men*. New York: Basic Books, pp. 229–51.

—— (1996) *Masculinity Reconstructed*. New York: Plume.

Littrell, J.M., Lee-Borden, N. and Lorenz, J. (1979) 'A developmental framework for counseling supervision', *Counselor Education and Supervision*, 19: 129–36.

Martin, J.S., Goodyear, R.K. and Newton, F.B. (1987) 'Clinical supervision: an intensive case study', *Professional Psychology: Research and Practice*, 18: 225–35.

Nelson, M.L. (1996) 'Separation vs. connection, the gender controversy: implications for counseling women', *Journal of Counseling and Development*, 74: 339–44.

—— (1997) 'An interactional model for the empowerment of women in supervision', *Counselor Education and Supervision*, 37: 125–39.

Nelson, M.L. and Holloway, E.L. (1990) 'Relation of gender to power and involvement in supervision', *Journal of Counseling Psychology*, 37: 473–81.

O'Neill, J.M. (1981) 'Patterns of gender role conflict and strain: sexism and fear of femininity in men's lives', *Personnel and Guidance Journal*, 60: 203–10.

O'Neill, J.M., Good, G.E. and Holmes, S. (1995) 'Fifteen years of theory and research on men's gender role conflict: new paradigms for empirical research', in R.F. Levant and W.S. Pollack (eds) *A New Psychology of Men*. New York: Basic Books, pp. 164–206.

Pleck, J. (1981) *The Myth of Masculinity*. Cambridge, MA: MIT Press.

Pollack, W.S. (1995) 'No man is an island: toward a new psychoanalytic psychology of men', in R.F. Levant and W.S. Pollack (eds) *A New Psychology of Men*. New York: Basic Books, pp. 33–67.

Sells, J.N., Goodyear, R.K., Lichtenberg, J.W. and Polkinghome, D.E. (1997) 'Relationship of supervisor and trainee gender to in-session verbal behavior and ratings of trainee skills', *Journal of Counseling Psychology*, 44: 406–12.

Stoltenberg, C. and Delworth, U. (1987) *Supervising Counselors and Therapists: A Developmental Approach*. San Francisco: Jossey-Bass.

3 Supervision and working with disability

Terri Spy and Caron Oyston

Caron remembers the following story well:

> At my Grandfather's funeral I remember the vicar talking to the family as they sat in the pews in tears. He was telling us something that seemed to make so much sense to me. I felt that it gave me real strength. It means so much more to me now and I hope that it will help you to understand me and this chapter more easily. The vicar spoke about my grandfather using his name, Bert, and recognized how loved he had been by all present. Yes he had, he had been a wonderful man, loving and giving, wise and kind. The vicar continued by saying that he was sure we would have loved him just as much if he had had no legs. What a strange thing to say! Of course we would have done, he was indeed a truly terrific guy. The vicar went on to say that we probably would even have loved him if he had had no legs nor any arms. What was this strange vicar saying? There would never be any doubt that we all loved Papa. It was then that the minister told us to carry on the loving as it was only Papa's body that had now gone and that his spirit was still with us. Of course it was, and still is.

It is now that I can more fully understand what his strange speech implied. When talking of 'disability', and the many people with disabilities, it seems that the thoughts go to that disability and not to the actual person at all. Yet it is with the person that we, as supervisors and as therapists, are working. Everybody has a body, but are not their bodies. Yes, we are all just living in this shell we call a body. Some say it is just a creature to live in. We all have a body of some shape or form, of various colours and sizes, and we are all unique because we are not our bodies but the very essence of our own being. We are individuals with hopes and dreams, goals and expectations – all singular and wonderful in our own ways. This is what we are trained to believe in our professional world. When one of these 'creatures' malfunctions in any sort of way the other 'creatures' find it difficult. Society suddenly grows attitudes, assumptions and prejudice.

The impact of disability in practice on all members of the supervisory triangle – supervisor, supervisee and client – is not an area which has been given much attention. Although there are a number of different definitions of supervision, we do not intend to offer another in this chapter. However, we do believe that a definition of disability is of the utmost importance. The terminology used to define 'disability' has been difficult to find from many of the official sources. We decided to focus on the most recent of these, the Disability Discrimination Act 1995 (DDA). It states that disability is *'a physical or mental impairment which has a substantial long-term adverse effect on a person's ability to carry out normal day-to-day activities'* (*The Definition of Disability* 1995: DL60). This, according to the Act, includes physical limitations affecting the senses such as sight and hearing. It also includes 'learning disabilities and mental illness recognised by a respected body of medical opinion'.

The Disability Discrimination Act 1995 (DDA) came into effect on 2 December 1996. This was meant to give people with disabilities 'the right not to be discriminated against in employment, the provision of goods, services and facilities and in the selling and letting of land'. It has had a good deal of opposition from many people with disabilities who claim that the DDA is flawed. It was the only official definition that we could use, to give as a starting point. The Act and its implications for others needs to be clarified. For example a respected body of medical opinion defines *'substantial'*, as 'the inability to turn taps or knobs'. *'Long-term* effects' can last at least 12 months or for the rest of the life of the person affected. The above definition of 'disability' is medically based (Figure 3.1) and there is no recognition of the social model of disability which is the way in which people are disabled by the structures and practices in society (Figure 3.2). It is our hope that with these models in mind we, as supervisors and counsellors, can explore and, where necessary, rectify our supervision practice and model of therapy-giving.

Visible and invisible

In society, 'the Disabled' seems to be the name that has been bestowed on all persons, men and women, who have one or more

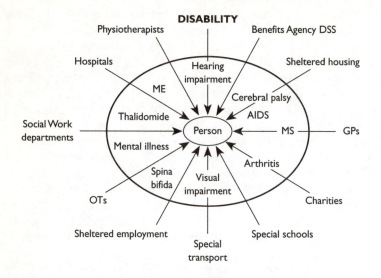

Figure 3.1   *Responses in society to a person's medical condition (Makin 1995)*

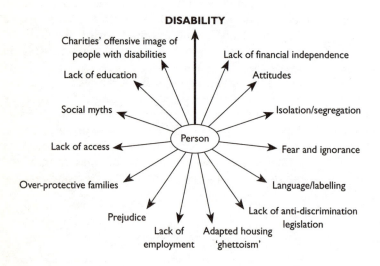

Figure 3.2   *It is the 'barriers' present in society that truly disable people (Makin 1995)*

limitation within their bodies. It is important to note that some people have had their disability since birth while others have acquired theirs later in life. This title is given very freely to those people who have more obvious limitations such as lost limbs or a white stick. People with less obvious disabilities, for example epilepsy, hearing loss, or dyslexia, are often not recognized at all. There can often be an intolerance, due to a lack of understanding, around invisible disabilities. All of us have limitations yet only those with obvious identifiable conditions are so labelled. As far as definitions of disability go, a high proportion of you reading this chapter will have your own definition of 'disability'. As defined within the medical model of disability people are seen and treated as their 'label', as Makin highlights (Figure 3.1 and 3.2).

For the purpose of this chapter it is also important to note that in the United Kingdom alone, there are more than 6,202,000 adults with disabilities, 14.5 per cent of the adult population. Of these, 93.2 per cent live in the community and the remainder live in institutions. It has also been suggested that one in four of the adult population will become disabled during their lifetime. Given such a high proportion of people with a disability, the question needs to be raised as to why so few of these are either clients, counsellors, psychotherapists or indeed supervisors.

Language

It is important for us to remember how language has the potential to be a tool of oppression, and how powerful this is for the oppressor, and how disempowering for people with a disability. Supervisors need to be aware of the impact and misuse of words used by their supervisees. Language, and the attitude that lies behind a particular misuse of words is clearly demonstrated by the term *'the disabled'*. By this term people with disabilities are clumped together as a collective noun comparable to 'the cars', 'the cows', 'the cats'. Another example is the use of the word 'handicap'. In fact this word comes from a fourteenth-century horse-racing term referring to riders with gifted horses who were required to ride with a cap in one hand. This term is offensive to many people with a disability as it implies begging. The word 'invalid' has two different meanings, the first as 'a person who is disabled or chronically ill', and the second as 'not valid because it has been based on a mistake' (*Collins English Dictionary* 1994). It is important to notice the impact of the misuse of these words and how oppressive they are to people.

Could this be one reason why people with a disability do not come into a therapeutic relationship or training? So often people with a disability are seen as 'different' or asexual. They cannot be seen for themselves, but rather as 'the MS woman' or 'the arthritic man', or 'that spastic'. They need to be addressed as 'a person with MS' or 'a person with arthritis' or 'a person who has cerebral palsy'. As supervisors it is of utmost importance that the language we use is a model for our supervisees and client group. The supervisor has a responsibility to provide a knowledge base of appropriate and non-offensive language when working with supervisees. Sometimes supervisees need to be aware of their use of language. If they have a tendency to describe a client, who has a disability, in negative terms, the supervisor needs to confront this. Counsellors working with persons with a disability need to be encouraged to look at *their* attitudes, prejudices and thoughts, as do we, as supervisors. It is the responsibility of the supervisor to encourage supervisees to explore these issues within the supervision context and within their own personal therapy as appropriate. This also applies to supervisors themselves.

The environment

In 1990 the government launched the 'two-tick' symbol for disability (see Figure 3.3). Use of this symbol by employers on their publicity material, recruitment literature, and so on was intended to indicate that they supported, and were willing to apply, the policies and practice to highlight their willingness to maintain a good minimum standard. In Figure 3.4 below we have used the two-tick symbol to demonstrate the complexity of the supervisory relationship. This is applicable when either the supervisor, supervisee or client has a disability or any combination within the supervisory triangle.

Much depends on the type of disability that any of these may experience. For example, if the supervisee is a wheelchair-user and the supervisor works in an upstairs room without access it is then unlikely that supervision can take place in this setting. The contract for supervision and the environment in which it takes

Figure 3.3   *The two-tick symbol for disability*

place will need to take this into account and may even require working with supervisees in their own home environment.

One example involves a client who was a wheelchair-user. Access was only available downstairs, while the counsellor's practice room was upstairs. In this case the counsellor contracted to work downstairs as there was only one step and there was also an accessible downstairs toilet. The counsellor also ensured that the lounge was devoid of personal items during the therapy sessions. The client did in fact use the toilet using the wheelchair. It should be noted here that the counsellor did not become aware until one year into the relationship that the client *was* able to climb the stairs (with assistance). This particular counsellor had assumed that this client was unable to do this. This clearly shows the importance of asking clients about their abilities and not making false assumptions. Thereafter the client climbed the stairs with assistance for the next one and a half years!

Another example is of a supervisee with multiple sclerosis who did not appear to have a disability in any form at the start of the contract. At this early stage her MS had not progressed into a mobility issue. The supervisee chose not to mention the diagnosis at this stage, thinking it quite irrelevant to her professional life. As individual supervision continued over the years so did the progression of the multiple sclerosis symptoms. She eventually disclosed the reason for her limping, and her inability to climb stairs. The supervisor was upset and concerned for what was happening

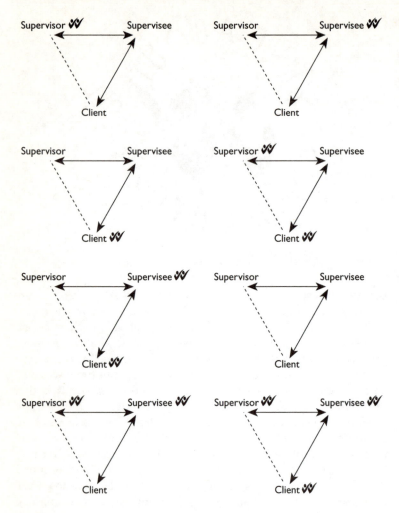

Figure 3.4   *Complexity of the supervisory relationship (adapted from Lago and Thompson's (1996) model)*

to her supervisee. The supervisee expressed frustration and anger that her illness was causing such difficulties. A new contract was negotiated for the supervision to take place in a downstairs room. The supervisee also participated in group supervision and more negotiation was needed with the other group members. This was to ensure that all group members could express their individual feelings and concerns. It also allowed discussion to be open and free-flowing in order for another new contract to be formed with the group. The outcome was that both individual and group supervision then occurred downstairs. In this context, we believe that it was the supervisor's responsibility to provide accessible accommodation.

The environment is of paramount importance to accommodate the physical needs of the person with disabilities with whom we are working. As we have mentioned earlier, not all disabilities are visible. This does not mean that the environment is less important. For a person with hearing limitations, background noise can be very distracting, and so it is significant when there is a washing machine rumbling away or there are roadworks outside. If the work takes place in an office setting, then it is the supervisor's responsibility to find room-space with a low noise level. Colour-blindness can bring it's own distractions. If the client or super-visee has difficulty distinguishing between the colours red and green, and the supervisor is wearing a red shirt while sitting on a green chair, the colours will blend together. This may mean that there could be a problem distinguishing one from the other! Thought will need to be given to seating and spacing if there is a hearing loss or a speech difficulty. A client using sign language, may need an interpreter during sessions. It is important to note, at this point, that any such assistance should be suggested by the client and not by the supervisor or counsellor. This ensures the boundaries of confidentiality for the person requesting such aid. It is possible, with appropriate training, for the counsellor to learn sign language as an adjunct to his or her practice.

As able-sighted people enter a room they absorb a great deal of information about the setting, colours, contours, pictures and furnishing. For a person with limited sight, it is useful to be given the opportunity to observe the new environment for a while longer in order to learn the layout. This promotes trust by demonstrating sensitivity and awareness of needs (but is not the usual practice within a totally able-bodied setting). Discussing such topics with clients can be sensitive and often difficult for counsellors. Super-vision can guide and teach the counsellor the skills required to ask the other person what steps may be taken to avoid hindering them any further.

When one of the writers asked a client what her needs were in relation to her disability, she was told, 'To be able to put my feet up or take off my shoes or sit with a cushion on my lap to rest my elbows, without feeling my actions are being assessed in any way.

To be asked which chair is best for me today, without a fuss.' Another client who had a childhood disability expressed the requirement for special seating. The chairs in the counsellor's room were satisfactory, but a further negotiation would have been necessary had they not been adequate. A supervisor/counsellor with a disability herself told how she was unable to go to meet her clients at the front door because of her mobility limitation. She decided to have a doorbell/intercom system installed which allows her to greet clients and supervisees when they arrive, and to open the door lock electronically (enabling the person to enter and come into the room used for her practice). This means that on initial contact the client/supervisee needs to be informed of the counsellor/supervisor's disability. It can have an impact and needs to be discussed openly in order for individuals (and group members) not to become rescuers/helpers. Such a discussion enables each supervisee to make their own choice as to whether or not they wish to work with this particular supervisor.

Supervisors need to be aware of their educational role. Holloway (1995: 188), quotes from The Association for Counsellor Education and Supervision Standards for Counsellor Supervision (ACES):

> The supervisor's primary functions are to teach the inexperienced counsellor and to foster their professional development, to serve as consultants to experienced counsellors, and to assist at all levels in the provision of effective counselling services.

Thus supervisors need to raise awareness of any discriminatory practices which may exist.

An important development is the use of the telephone for counselling and supervision. This is particularly useful for people who have severe mobility difficulties. Contracting for this mode of work is facilitated in exactly the same way as for all professional work. These are just a few of the issues which can confuse therapeutic boundaries for both counsellors and supervisors.

Contracting

An example of supervisory contracting is given by Compton (1987), whose Supervisory Learning Contract (SLC) covers the following areas:

1. purpose of the supervision
2. expectations regarding clients

3. expectations regarding agency
4. format for presentations
5. supervision schedule
6. time frame
7. location and setting
8. taping expectations
9. evaluation process
10. fees and payment.

We would suggest that this contract can be applied when working with people with disabilities, particularly within the areas of location and setting (7). A supervisee or client with mobility limitations will need to be advised about locality and given information such as accessible parking. This is equally important within the supervisee/client relationship. Supervisors/supervisees need to be willing to contract with supervisees/clients to offer support in helping them from their vehicle into the practice room. This may take many forms, such as bag-carrying, wheelchair-pushing, elbow-holding. The individual may also require help in getting up steps, viewing the room, seating, and with whatever other needs they may have. Remember always to ask what help or support is required. Clients are usually happy to state their needs. One example of this was a client with limited sight who asked if the psychotherapist would hold his elbow and guide him. The response was, 'I think you should learn to be independent. Anyway I don't touch clients.' How would a supervisor use supervision in this context? Or might he or she subtly reinforce this behaviour?

Most supervisees need to explain to their supervisor their disability and such things as access before they are able to contract to work. This will be additional to the usual supervision contract. The need for such knowledge, awareness and negotiating skills will be something not every supervisor may have considered. Awareness of these facts can only reinforce the importance of our work.

Training

There is no specific counselling or psychotherapy training for people with disabilities, as there is no training for supervisors with disabilities. All are expected to fit into an able-bodied environment and to adapt according to their personal needs. The

British Association for Counselling (BAC) has set up a working group on disability issues, which is now called the Committee for Disability Issues (CDI). This is a specific group for exploration into issues surrounding disability, whether of counsellors, clients or supervisors. The number of trained counsellors and supervisors with a disability is not known to the writers, and access to this information is not available. At the present time it is our understanding that the majority of counsellors and supervisors have been trained within an able-bodied setting.

We would recommend Carroll's book, *Counselling Supervision: Theory, Skills and Practice* (1996: Chapter 2), which explores the trends and debates involved in moving from counselling to educational models of supervision. The author highlights a model curriculum for counselling supervision training which has six domains. We would suggest that the second, 'Reviewing issues within supervision such as: power, gender, cross-cultural counselling and supervision' (1996: 32), could also include disability awareness. Ideally, all training should include this awareness. At the moment, it is difficult to recommend a particular supervisor training model in this context, not so much because of the complexity of issues but rather because the lack of awareness on the part of supervisors to the importance of the issues. Much supervisor training tends to lump together most issues, such as ageism, sexism, gender, disability, and others, as if they were one and the same. They are not.

Although many of the issues for people with a disability are the same as those for able-bodied persons, many supervisors require separate training on aspects such as access, mobility, and resources available. Organizations such as Disability Matters provide training packages to meet a variety of training needs. BAC is planning to create the new BAC Disability Resources Pack, giving BAC and its membership a publication on disability issues fit for the twenty-first century. Unison, the union for public sector workers, has a National Disabled Members Committee (NDMC) which tackles discrimination faced by its members with disabilities. It also provides training for stewards which could be useful for supervisors (see contact numbers at the end of this chapter). Useful reading material is in short supply for supervision training. However, that does not mean that the issue of disability should be put aside because of a perceived small uptake. The issue is too important for this attitude.

Case study

This case illustration is of (a) a client presenting to a counsellor and (b) the counsellor presenting issues in supervision. Client J. is aged 28 years. She is a white female studying for a diploma in counselling, at a venue which has limited access. She broke her back in a freak accident and is now paraplegic. She is a wheelchair user, can self-propel and is able to transfer from wheelchair to seating and back. She also drives her own car. However, the counselling training takes place in an upstairs room, and there is no wheelchair access. Some weeks into her personal counselling relationship (a mandatory part of her training) she became very distressed. She said that she was considering leaving her training because of difficulties in 'always having to remind tutors about her personal needs'. She could 'just cope' with getting herself (on her bottom) up a flight of stairs. What she found particularly upsetting was being left at mealtimes when her peers and tutors went for tea or lunch. Her fear of accidents, and even the possibility of fire, distracted her from her learning. She believed that she would be forgotten. The counsellor focused on her fears and anxieties about being left and wondered if this had happened to her as a child. The counsellor also shared in an appropriate self-disclosure of her own fear of fire.

When the counsellor presented for supervision her agenda involved the difficulties her client appeared to have in stating her needs. She could not understand her client's anger. She told her supervisor that, in fact, her peers *did* help her to carry items up the stairs, including her wheelchair.

The supervisor needed to explore with the supervisee what her understanding of disability was, in order to clarify how the client's disability impacted on her. This was determined through the use of a 'Systems Approach Model' (Holloway 1995, Figure 3.5 and 3.6). The supervisor, through the use of the *function* 'consulting', combined with the *task* of 'emotional awareness in supervisory relationship', enabled the supervisor to resolve this professional situation by seeking the information and opinions of the supervisee. The 'consulting' enabled the supervisor to stay aware of her responsibility for both supervisee *and* client, while at the same time offering her the support initiated in the contracting. By using the *teaching task* of 'emotional awareness' the supervisor was able to complete this part of the process. In order to inform the supervisor's work there was a need to get rapid feedback on the two relationships, the counsellor and her client, and the supervisee and her supervisor, thus sustaining the *invisible link* between client and supervisor.

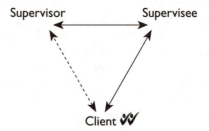

Figure 3.5   *Extract from Figure 3.4*

> **Emotional Awareness** refers to the supervisee's self-awareness of feelings, thoughts and actions that result from working with the client and with the supervisor. Many theories of counselling stress the importance of understanding one's own emotional material both historically as well as immediately with the client. The participants' emotional responses in the relationship of supervision may also be an important subject for their work with the client. (Holloway 1995: 24)

The combined use of the above *task* and *function* enabled both supervisor and supervisee to see quite clearly that she was feeling a little afraid of addressing the issue of disability with her client. With this now in the foreground the supervisor felt able to make use of another of the tasks 'counselling skills' and offer the supervisee *empathy*. Through the use of this task the supervisor was able to remain in the supervisee's internal frame of reference and recognize and acknowledge her anxiety. This task helped the supervisor to focus on what action to suggest she take with her client.

From this place, having clarified this issue, the supervisor raised the question of whether or not the supervisee had missed the client's real issues of lack of dignity, respect and access rights. Other topics discussed were how the issues of power and control – or lack of them – had impacted upon the client's needs, and whether the counsellor could appropriately support the client in meeting her needs while maintaining the boundaries of counselling. The supervisor used another of the functions, 'instructing and advising' to encourage the supervisee to be open with her client and to disclose her new-found knowledge base around disabilities.

> The **Instructing and Advising** function consists of the supervisor's providing information, opinions, and suggestions based on professional knowledge and skill. According to process research in supervision, this dominant pattern of interaction is an *instructing and advising behaviour* by the supervisor followed by the trainee's [supervisee's] agreement with, or encouragement of, the supervisor who is giving advice. (Holloway 1995: 34)

Holloway and Poulin (1995) have characterized this as a 'teacher–student' function. Subsequently, the supervisor suggested some training for the counsellor in rights for people with disabilities.

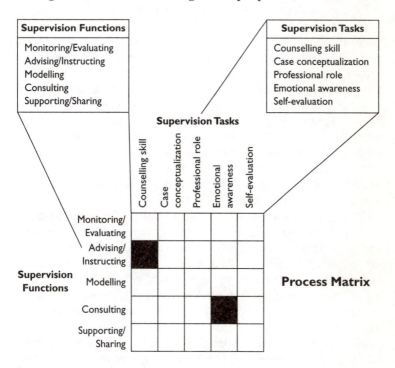

Figure 3.6   *The tasks and functions of supervision (Holloway 1995. Reprinted with permission of Sage Publications, Inc.)*

The three main issues for the counsellor revolved around firstly, her interpretation of the client's issues, that is, appropriate access. The second issue concerned her knowledge of disability and how oppression and discrimination may occur. The third issue concerned the roles adopted by the counsellor in respect of the client while maintaining appropriate professional boundaries. It is important for the supervisor to have knowledge of a wide range of therapeutic approaches. One-dimensional supervision and counselling would not have helped the client. A balance of various counselling theories being put into practice is what is required.

Summary and concluding comments

When working with supervisees, whose clients may have a disability or limitations affecting them, supervisors need to remain aware of another dimension to their model of supervision. The majority of people have limited experience in treating people with a disability in a holistic manner. Often through ignorance, fear or prejudice, discriminatory barriers develop which may further trap a person with disabilities. Supervisors and supervisees should be mindful that the problems which the client experiences may not always appear on the surface. The two models of disabilities referred to by Makin (1995) (Figures 3.1 and 3.2) highlight how these potentially discriminatory practices can occur. Supervisors need to remain conscious of discrimination shown to people with disabilities because of how society is organized, and the language that is often used to oppress.

Although it appears that the Disability Discrimination Act (DDA) of 1995 was meant to give people with disabilities the right not to be discriminated against, the argument continues. According to Andrew Smith, the Minister for Employment and Disabled Peoples Rights, the UK government is committed to 'a truly inclusive society with full and enforceable civil rights for all people'. According to Unison (1997), 'further lobbies are being organised by the "Rights Now" consortium until such time as civil rights for disabled people are won and the DDA is dumped'. There is concern that the Act is ambiguous and needs to be more clearly defined around words such as 'substantial' and 'progressive condition'.

Earlier in this chapter we asked the question why, given the high proportion of people with a disability, so few of these are either clients, counsellors, psychotherapists or indeed supervisors. Given the apparent lack of training in this area both for able-bodied people and the few disabled professionals, it is not surprising that there are such small numbers. Training partners and teams that consist of colleagues who are themselves disabled and culturally different need to become accepted in practice as an epitome of a useful role-model. This would represent the complexity of data that needs to be addressed within training.

Nancy Boyd-Franklin (1989) made a strong case for the empowerment of therapists (counsellors) through training in order that they may also empower their clients. The concept of client empowerment has always been an aim in counselling in general. It is clear that Boyd-Franklin is concerned to explore how trainee therapists or counsellors might be enabled to mobilize all their potential for working skilfully and sensitively in transcultural therapeutic settings. The writers of this chapter believe that this ideal should also be usefully employed as standard practice within training in general, because it is so usual that supervision is provided by able-bodied supervisors. The ideal should also be applied whilst working within any part of the supervisory triangles described in Figure 3.4.

The setting in which supervisors and supervisees work needs to be accessible for all groups of people. It is likely that it is the posture of society itself that constitutes the most disabling part of being a person with disabilities, rather than the physical effects of the person's condition. On the whole, it is the environment, and how it is constructed physically, and the attitudes of individuals within it, that result in certain persons being disabled. People with limitations are people with *different* abilities and requirements, yet who can be further disabled by a society that is geared to the needs of those who can walk, have good sight and hearing, can speak distinctly, and are intellectually dextrous. We need to consider our working environment and to extend this to training establishments and all centres that offer professional development in any form. It is important to realize that this is not a case of researching the numbers of attendees with disabilities and then finding appropriate accommodation. It is about accepting that anybody attending, whatever the situation, has a right of total access and is not further disabled by poorly designed buildings.

We have given one example of contracting that we felt could be applied when working with people with disabilities. The writers are aware that there are many forms of contracting which can apply in this situation. However, the most important aspect is the negotiation between all corners of the supervisory triangle where there is an issue of disability and of the use of language applicable in this situation.

For any of us as supervisors working with disability, remember that we are either healing or harming. There is no in-between. Therefore, even in our supervision, we should be practising healing. As supervisors of others' work we need to be constructive, supportive, guiding, training, and to monitor and evaluate our commitment. We would encourage readers to fulfil these expectations successfully, responsibly and respectfully.

Useful organisations include:

Access Committee for England, Unit 12, City Forum, 250 City Road, London EC1V 8AF: tel. 0171 250 0008

Arthritis Care, 18 Stephenson Way, London NW1 2HD: tel. 0171 916 1500

Association of Disabled Professionals, 170 Benton Hill, Horbury, Wakefield, West Yorkshire WF4 5HW: tel. 01924 270335

British Association for Counselling, 1 Regent Place, Rugby, Warwickshire CV21 2PJ: tel. 01788 578328 (Information Line)

British Council of Disabled People, Unit 14, De Bradlei House, Chapel Street, Belper, Derby DE56 1AR: tel. 01773 828182

Computability Centre, PO Box 94, Warwick CV34 5WS: tel. 0800 269545

Disability Matters Ltd, Berkeley House, West Tytherley, Salisbury, Wiltshire SP5 1NF: tel. 01794 341144

Disability Resource Team, Bedford House, 125–133 Camden High Street, London NW1 7JR: tel. 0171 482 4826

Employers Forum on Disability, Nutmeg House, 60 Gainsford Street, London SE1 2NY: tel. 0171 403 3020

Employment Service, Disability Services Placement Assessment and Counselling Team, 3rd Floor, Rockingham Court, Rockingham Street, Sheffield S1 4EB: tel. 0114 203300

Greater London Association For Disabled People: tel. 0171 346 5800

MENCAP, Royal Society for People with Learning Disabilities, 123 Golden Lane, London EC1Y 0RT: tel. 0171 454 0454

MIND, National Association for Mental Health, 22 Harley Street, London W1N 2ED: tel. 0171 637 0741

Multiple Sclerosis Society, 25 Effie Road, Fulham, London SW6 1EE: tel. 0171 610 7171

Opportunities for People with Disabilities, 1 Bank Buildings, Princes Street, London EC2R 8EU: tel. 0171 726 4963

Royal Association for Disability and Rehabilitation (RADAR), 12 City Forum, 250 City Road, London EV1V 8AF: tel. 0171 250 3222

Royal National Institute for the Blind, 224 Great Portland Street, London W1N 6AA: tel. 0171 388 1266

Royal National Institute for Deaf People, 19–23 Featherstone Street, London EC1Y 8SL: tel. 0171 296 8000

Scope, 16 Fitzroy Square, London W1P 6LP: tel. 0171 387 9571

The Terrence Higgins Trust, 52 Gray's Inn Road, London WC1X 8JU: tel. 0171 831 0330

TYPETALK, The National Telephone Relay Service, Pauline Ashley House, Ravenside Retail Park, Speke Road, Liverpool L24 8QB: tel. 0151 709 9494

Unison Headquarters, 1 Madledon Place, London WC1H 9AJ: tel. 0181 854 2244

References

Boyd-Franklin, N. (1989) *Black Families in Therapy: A Multisystems Approach*. New York: Guilford Press.

British Association for Counselling (1996/1997) *Annual Report*. Rugby: BAC Publications.

Carroll, M. (1996) *Counselling Supervision: Theory, Skills and Practice*. London: Cassell.

Compton, J.R. (1987) 'The Supervisory Learning Context' in B.K. Estadt, J.R. Compton and M.C. Blancette (eds) *The Art of Clinical Supervision*. New Jersey: Paulist Press.

The Definition of Disability (1995) London: HMSO Publications.

Disability Matters Ltd (1994) Delegate notes.

Holloway, E. (1995) *Clinical Supervision: A Systems Approach*. Thousand Oaks, CA: Sage.

Holloway, E.L. and Poulin, K. (1995) 'Discourse in supervision', in J. Siegried (ed.) *Therapeutic and Everyday Discourse as Behavior Change: Towards a Micro-analysis in Psychotherapy Process Research*. New York: Ablex.

Houston, G. (1990) *Supervision and Counselling*: London: Rochester Foundation Publications.

Lago, C. and Thompson, J. (1996) *Race, Culture and Counselling*. Buckingham: Open University Press.

Makin, T. (1995) 'The social model of disability', *Counselling* (The Journal of the BAC), 6 (4): 274.

Unison (1997) *Focus* Fortnightly Paper for Stewards, 62 (18 July).

4 Supervision and sexual orientation

Paul Hitchings

The effect of differences in sexual orientation within the supervisory triad approximates a cross-cultural situation which can have a significant impact on the supervisory process. The literature on cross-cultural issues in counselling and supervision can be very helpful in illuminating many of these pertinent areas.

Brown and Landrum-Brown (1996: 267–8) in their examination of this perspective in counsellor supervision note:

> To the extent that any supervisory triad member differs on any salient feature from the general population, the content, process, and outcome of supervision can be negatively affected. . . . A supervisor, supervisor/ counselor, and client may come from cultural groups that may experience different degrees of separation and oppression than are experienced in the general society. Those experiences shape one's general views and rules about life and how to approach living in it. In other words, the experiences influence one's level of acculturation. Culture based perspectives may be so fundamentally different that effective supervision involving the supervisory parties is obstructed. Cultural differences may be reflected in assessed levels of acculturation, perceptions of oppression and unfair discrimination, confidence in societal institutions (like counsellor training and supervision), and worldviews.

Sexual orientation is a salient feature of difference. However, it is a difference unlike race, class and other more visible factors, in that it can by individuals be revealed, partially revealed (for example, we both know this about me, but the rule is that it doesn't get mentioned) or can be kept effectively and totally hidden. To further complicate matters there are also degrees of positioning along a hetero–homosexual continuum that individuals might choose to place themselves. Both of these characteristics of sexual orientation create a potential complexity in the supervisory triad (client, supervisee and supervisor). In this chapter, for the sake of clarity a somewhat simplified description of the more complex possibilities will be used.

Gay affirmative supervision

This philosophy asserts that lifestyles other than those of 100 per cent heterosexuality are equally valid. In other words that homosexuality and heterosexuality are normal variations of human sexuality, and that instead homophobia in the person (client/supervisee), other (supervisor) and institution/society become the focus of the work. (For a wider discussion see Krajeski 1986; Maylon 1982; Davies 1996.)

Lesbian, gay and bisexual people still experience a considerable level of prejudice and discrimination in all avenues of society. Despite significant societal changes over the last two decades, a text such as this is still likely to be considered by some as controversial. The position of a gay affirmative philosophy taken in this chapter is set in the context of a professional culture that is still considerably homophobic. In support of this latter statement the reader is invited to consider the following few examples.

- Despite the fact that mental health professionals in the USA officially rejected homosexuality as a psychological disorder in 1973 (American Psychiatric Association 1990) and in 1975 the American Psychological Association adopted a gay affirmative policy (CLGC 1986; Morin and Rothblum 1991), there still exists amongst American psychologists a group called the National Association for Research and Therapy of Homosexuality (NARTH) who assert that homosexuality can be treated by addressing 'unwanted' homosexual feelings (*APA Monitor* 1996).
- Within the British Psychological Society attempts to form a Psychology of Lesbianism have met with repeated refusals (Beloff 1993) and twice a proposal to establish a Section for Lesbian and Gay Psychology has met a similar fate (Coyle et al. 1995). However, at the time of writing (February 1998), the proposal seems likely to succeed at the third attempt.
- As recently as 1995, Professor Charles Socarides a well-known psychoanalyst from the USA, who believes that all homosexuals should be treated and cured, was invited to the UK, to address the Association for Psychoanalytical Psychotherapists in the NHS (Samuels 1995)
- It remains difficult for lesbian and gay students to enrol on psychoanalytic training courses in the UK. Davies (1996) quotes Ellis (1994) as follows: 'found in her research into psychoanalytically oriented training establishments in Britain

that, in spite of reluctance to admit to refusing admission to a programme because someone was lesbian or gay, she had evidence of heterosexist bias, beliefs that homosexuality equated with psychopathology, and the fact that an "out" lesbian or gay man would be regarded as "too political" and therefore "inappropriate" for training.'

- A vitriolic letter by a Fellow of the British Psychological Society published in *The Psychologist* in response to an academic article in the previous issue on lesbian and gay relationships: 'I object to the misleading use in a publication of a scientific society of the innocent-sounding word "gay" when referring to what is the abnormal practice of anal intercourse between males' (*The Psychologist* 1995).

Perhaps these few examples are sufficient to alert the reader that a significant minority in the helping professions does not share the stance of a gay affirmative approach to counselling and supervision.

In common with other societally sanctioned oppressive attitudes it is likely that we all (including gay and lesbian individuals) retain some remnants of belief in heterosexual supremacy, while at the same time genuinely wanting to alter this belief and associated attitudes. This requires fully embracing a non-pathological stance and a philosophy that holds an equality of validity for those individuals who might describe their sexuality as falling somewhere else along the human sexuality continuum than the socially prescribed norm of 100 per cent heterosexuality.

A gay affirmative stance is a deeply held value, that homosexual, bisexual and heterosexual identities/behaviours are all equally valid and that all these sexualities are derived from the normal range of human sexuality. Additionally, in my view, such a stance needs to be evidently congruent with beliefs, attitudes and behaviours of the practitioner in both their professional and private lives.

Core concepts

While it is not the intention in this chapter to develop further the information and ideas that is readily available elsewhere (for example, Davies 1996; Hitchings 1997) on working with lesbian, gay and bisexual people, nevertheless a brief résumé of central issues/concepts may be helpful. Where relevant, implications for the supervisory process are also referred to before being elaborated on later in the chapter.

Terminology

I have for the most part used the term 'homosexual' throughout this chapter. This does carry the risk of marginalizing or rendering lesbian women and bisexuals invisible, and has the danger of perpetuating negative historical associations. It also does not distinguish between a sexual act and a chosen identity. There are, in addition, the problems of historically inherited terms such as the previously referred to 'gay affirmative' concept. Despite these problems, the term 'homosexual', for the purposes of writing this chapter, is considerably less cumbersome and I believe the context provided corrects for any ambiguity the word alone may possess.

How do we define sexual orientation?

This seemingly simple question is a complex one to answer. Most people would not regard someone who had a singular homosexual experience as homosexual. However, what of the individual whose behaviour is heterosexual, is deeply emotionally attached to their opposite-sex partner and who yearns to be with someone of the same sex? Is this person homosexual? These are difficult considerations and reveal the complexity of even defining an individual's sexual orientation. The prevailing definition in a given instance has social, scientific, therapeutic and political implications. The incidence of bisexuality has been largely ignored in our society by the polarizing of human sexualities into two simplistic, discrete groups of either homo- or heterosexual. This is despite the fact that bisexuality is considerably more common than exclusive homosexuality. Kinsey (Kinsey et al. 1948), for example, found that 37 per cent of males had experienced homosexual orgasm at some point since adolescence, with an additional 13 per cent admitting to homosexual feelings which they had not acted upon. The figure of exclusive male homosexuality was 10 per cent for at least three years and 4 per cent throughout their lives. The figures for women were lower but the same argument is supported. Similar results have been reported in subsequent surveys (Gebhard 1972; Meyer 1985; Sell et al. 1990).

Coleman (1985) suggests categories that take into account not only behaviour but also fantasy and emotional attachments. Garnets and Kimmel (1991) suggest individuals may be presumed to be lesbian or gay if their primary affectional/erotic attachments are to people of the same gender, bisexual if their affectional/erotic attachments are to both men and women, and heterosexual when their primary affectional/erotic attachments are to members of the opposite gender. Davies (1996), emphasizes self-definition as the definitive factor. He differentiates between homosexual behaviour (an instance or repeated instance of sexual activity with a same-sex partner – perhaps ongoing in their life) and homosexual identity (self-definition as homosexual).

Ultimately all categories are simplifications and each person has a unique sexuality that may be fluid over time. However, in the context of a still homophobic and heterosexist society, I believe such simplification is both necessary and useful since naming helps to symbolize experience and allows the outlining of issues that are pertinent to dynamics that may be present in the supervisory triad. Although some of the complexity and richness can be lost I shall for the sake of clarity continue to use the dichotomous classification of homo and heterosexual, while reminding the reader of the risks involved.

The above discussion underlines the need to recognize that issues pertinent to sexual orientation do not only apply to those who identify as lesbian, gay or bisexual, but also to others – who form a much larger percentage of the population – whose behaviour or fantasies either do not fit given labels or who may be struggling with accepting a sexual identity. We need then to bear in mind a number of 'groupings'; (a) those whose entire behaviour and fantasies are 100 per cent homosexual; (b) those whose behaviour/fantasies have on occasions been to some extent homosexual; (c) those whose behaviour/fantasies might warrant a bisexual identity; and (d) those that more clearly are homosexual and may have chosen an identity congruent with this sexual orientation. Clearly members of the supervisory triad may be made up of any potential combination of the above groupings.

Homophobia

An early usage of this term by Weinberg (1972) defined it as 'the dread of being in close quarters with homosexuals – and in the case of homosexuals themselves, self loathing'. Hudson and Ricketts (1980) both enlarge the definition to include responses such as anxiety, unease, anger and fear while limiting the term to responses experienced by heterosexual towards homosexual people. This term has an individual focus and consequently other terms have been argued for which more clearly reflect the cultural/ societal frame such as 'anti-gay prejudice' (Herek 1991). The latter point also serves as a reminder that homophobia is deeply institutionalized in our society in a myriad of ways that might not easily be noticed by heterosexual people or even at times by homosexual people themselves. Davies (1996) offers a wider discussion of this issue. Of particular interest here is the way that homophobia may be institutionalized within the theories, models and practices of counselling. Here, for instance, theories of child development, models of healthy adult development and adjustment, assessment criteria, degree of counsellor disclosure, lack of awareness of interpersonal dynamics, for example a sexualized transference, may all play a part in maintaining a counselling culture that unwittingly supports homophobia.

Heterosexism

This is an equivalent term to institutionalized homophobia and defined by Blumenfeld and Raymond (1988: 244) as 'the system by which heterosexuality is assumed to be the only acceptable and viable life option'. Similarly Morin (1977) defined heterosexual bias 'as the belief system that values heterosexuality as superior to and/or more natural or normal than lesbian and gay sexual orientations' (quoted in Greene 1994: 629). As discussed above under the heading of homophobia our culture is deeply embedded within a heterosexist assumption, as evidenced in our social structures.

Internalized homophobia

In contrast to the definition of homophobia, internalized homophobia is usually used to denote the internalization of homophobic attitudes by homosexual persons. An individual growing up in a homophobic culture will almost certainly internalize such attitudes and values. Shidlo (1994: 178) defines the term as 'a set of negative attitudes and affects towards homosexual features in oneself. These features include same gender sexual and affectional feelings; same gender sexual behavior; same gender intimate relationships; and self labeling as lesbian, gay or homosexual.' This is a core concept for supervisors and counsellors to be aware of when working with lesbian, gay or bisexual clients and the more subtle manifestations require a high degree of awareness in counsellor and supervisor if collusion is to be avoided.

Coming out

This is the intra- and interpersonal psychological process by which individuals who are struggling to come to terms with a gay or lesbian identity in a homonegative society move to developing an increasingly healthy self-concept.

> 'Coming Out' involves a complex process of intra- and interpersonal transformations often beginning in adolescence and extending well into adulthood which lead to, accompany, and follow the events associated with acknowledgement of one's sexual orientation. The events are the external manifestations of an internal process of identity formation in a gay or lesbian person. (Hanley-Hackenbruck 1989: 21)

Cohen and Stein (1986: 32) define the term as follows:

> Coming out refers to a complicated developmental process which involves at a psychological level a person's awareness and acknowledgement of homosexual thoughts and feelings. For some persons, coming out ultimately leads to public identification as a gay man or lesbian.

Space does not permit a full exploration of the many models of the developmental process that have been formulated over the last two decades. The interested reader is referred to Davies (1996: Chapter 3) who offers a useful comparison of three different models, as well as a discussion of some of the factors that influence the resolution of this process. Hitchings (1997) also offers a detailed discussion of one of the models.

The supervisory situation

Helping the supervisee develop a contextual awareness

Certain contextual understandings are essential if the counsellor is to work effectively with homosexual clients. While many are elaborated on in texts aimed primarily at counsellors (referenced below) a brief résumé of some of the important issues is given here. The supervisor is in a position to aid the supervisee in developing such knowledge so that he/she can work effectively with this client group.

DIAGNOSIS AND ASSESSMENT OF THE CLIENT   Here the supervisor needs to be alert to the stage of the 'coming out' process of the client and how this provides a particular context within which particular client behaviours may need to be viewed. Gonsiorek (1985: 11) warned of the issues here:

> Paranoia and other florid reactions of a sexual identity crisis in a genuinely homosexual person are more likely to be partially, or at times completely, reality-based, as a result of severe interpersonal rejection, physical or sexual assault, impending or actual loss of job or a host of other possible ways in which a person may be traumatised because he or she is homosexual.

The above underlines the need to maintain the context of sexual orientation as background for presenting problems and has implications for the supervision of assessment and treatment direction being utilized. Potential issues for the supervisor to be alert to in the client are: depression (Davies 1996), alcohol and drug addiction (Kowszun and Malley 1996) and suicidal ideation (Remafedi et al. 1991), since these issues occur in higher frequency amongst homosexual people. Conversely, with clients presenting with such issues the possibility that they may be struggling with a homosexual identity must at least be considered.

Other examples of the altered meaning of certain issues when placed within a homosexual context, include particularly behaviour within relationships. For gay men, sex outside the relationship usually has a considerably lower emotional significance than for their heterosexual counterparts (Kitzinger and Coyle 1995). Harry (1983) estimates that 50 per cent of gay men, 30 per cent of lesbians and only 1 per cent of heterosexuals, in relationship of five years or more, choose to live apart. Without the context the counsellor could easily make inaccurate hypotheses, for example around a commitment issue. Simon (1996) presents useful material for working with homosexual couples and underlines the problems involved in transferring heterosexual models on to homosexual relationships.

The relationship between supervisor and supervisee

There are certain common tasks that the supervisor is likely to need to attend to particularly where the supervisee is heterosexual and the client homosexual. These are listed and discussed below.

ATTENDING TO TRANSFERENCE ISSUES   If the supervisee is homosexual and the supervisor heterosexual the expectation of shaming is likely to be quite high and consequent defences against that will likely be in operation. However, this situation also carries with it the possibility of a reparative experience for the supervisee, if the supervisor consistently offers a gay affirmative supervisory stance. This in turn is likely to strengthen the supervisory alliance.

ATTENDING TO COUNTERTRANSFERENCE ISSUES   These include the maintenance of stereotypical assumptions by either the counsellor towards the client or the supervisor towards the supervisee and/or the client. The task then of the supervisor is not only to be alert to the supervisee's countertransference but also to maintain an awareness of his/her own process. Davies (1996) argues: 'Where both consultant and therapist are heterosexual there is a need for the consultant to have some training in cross-cultural issues and to be aware that they are listening through their own "cultural filters".' He follows by offering suggestions made by Tievsky (1988: 58) of indicators that consultants (supervisors) pay particular attention to, in order to aid supervisees in their awareness,

> Some of the clues that researchers have determined as indicators of the existence of homophobia include joking about it (Gramick 1983), uneasiness (Moses and Hawkins 1982), hostility, stereotyping and denial (Messing et al. 1984) and exaggerating the significance of the client's orientation (Rabin et al. 1986), and of course pity (Woodman and Lenna 1980). Another indicator frequently found among professional psychotherapists is the attitude that sexual orientation makes absolutely no difference, thus ignoring the impact of life in a rejecting society. (Messing et al. 1984)

Samuels (1997) addresses an under-discussed potential source of countertransference, that of the potential jealousy of the homosexual by the heterosexual person. He noted that likely sources of such jealousy may emanate from the wider sexual freedom available in the homosexual subculture and the financial freedom that arises from the (usual but not always), absence of costs of child rearing.

ELICITING CLARITY OF VALUES   This is more than a belief in non-discrimination and there is a continuum from very negative attitudes to increasingly positive ones – for example see Appendix (page 78). Some counsellors may well be supportive of lesbian/gay clients generally but hold reservations about aspects of equality, for example the upbringing of children in a homosexual household, the right to equality on the age of consent for sexual relations, etc. Often on some of these examples homophobic attitudes remain even within an otherwise generally liberal framework. It is essential that supervisors are clear about their positioning on such a dimension, further their own awareness to create the possibility of change and aid their supervisees in developing such clarity.

CONFRONTING HOMOPHOBIC COLLUSION   This overlaps with the two previous issues of value system and countertransference. While the grosser examples are usually recognized by supervisees themselves, supervisors may need to help more actively with subtler forms by appropriate confrontation of the supervisee. An example of this latter category that could easily go unnoticed is offered below:

> Client: [previously married, now in a gay relationship] I'm so happy that both my children have turned out all right. . . . They're both now married and I have the pleasure of my grandchildren.
> Counsellor: You're really pleased that you parented them well.

Clearly here the supervisor has the task of helping the supervisee understand some of the subtleties of collusion in the counselling process. The task in such an example would be to help the supervisee understand how such a surface reflection, without any confrontation, colludes with an internalized negative view of homosexuality; it is also to challenge the implicit belief that homosexuality is 'caused' by a parenting error and the idea that homosexual people can't have children. They can and do. Further there may also be room to point out the different richness that would have occurred in the parent–child relationship had one of the children identified as homosexual. It is to be hoped that the analysis of even such a brief interchange shows the subtlety with which homophobic collusion can be reinforced.

SHOWING SENSITIVITY TO POWER ISSUES This, particularly, refers to the situation where the supervisor is heterosexual and the supervisee homosexual. Especially while the supervisee is in training supervisors often have an evaluative role. This can of course heighten transference issues and affect openness in the supervisory relationship and especially in the more psychoanalytic trainings. Supervisors need to be particularly sensitive in such situations, offer assurances where appropriate, and model a professional role that is exemplary in non-discriminatory practice.

SUPERVISOR FACILITATING OPENNESS WITHIN THE SUPERVISORY RELATIONSHIP Without openness it is likely that the interpersonal processes between supervisor and supervisee will detract from the central tasks of supervision. Where the supervisor is homosexual, and this is made overt, there is the opportunity for any issues the supervisee has to emerge (they may well further submerge, but I believe that in a generally good supervisory relationship this is unlikely). Where the supervisor is heterosexual and the supervisee is homosexual, general modelling of non-discriminatory practice, and knowledge by the supervisee of your value system will facilitate disclosure when appropriate in the supervisee.

AVOIDING MINIMIZING THE SIGNIFICANCE This often involves an over-emphasis on the intra-psychic dynamics and fails to address sexual orientation as a political issue. The illusion of 'it doesn't make a difference' clearly has the equivalent in the race arena of colour blindness. An 'orientation-blind' attitude, while possibly meant as a way of avoiding prejudice, carries the almost inevitable risk of perpetuating it. In parallel with the issues of race, Marsella and Pedersen (1981) identified three types of racial reaction – the illusion of colour blindness, the 'great white father' syndrome, and the assumption that all black people's problems revolve around the issues of being black. These potential pitfalls readily translate to sexual orientation.

AVOIDING EXAGGERATING THE SIGNIFICANCE This of course is the equivalent in the racial arena of attributing all problems to being black. While there may be some explanatory value in recognizing the contribution being homosexual has to an individual's current problems such an approach can easily provide a false sense of comfort in either the supervisee or supervisor. Significant understandings may be overlooked and the client's sense of shame compounded.

Maintaining an awareness of wider cultural context   The models and concepts of gay affirmative therapy are embedded largely within a western white value base. Issues can take on a significantly different perspective within a different cultural context, for example some Asian or African subcultures where the concept of the family as a unit has a significance that outweighs the western emphasis on individualism.

Scenarios for discussion

Thompson (1991) developed a series of triangular diagrams to conceptualize the potential issues across racial/cultural difference. Similarly these are employed here in the context of sexual orientation, although we need to bear in mind that they create a very artificial simplification by utilizing the false dichotomous division into heterosexual and homosexual and with an assumed openness when this may not be the case. Nevertheless, as long as this is clearly borne in mind, they do offer a structure to aid our conceptualization of the likely issues.

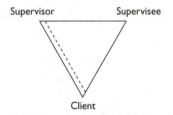

Figure 4.1   *The supervisory relationship (Lago and Thompson 1997: 122)*

Lago and Thompson (1997: 122) note the training potential offered: 'Taking one diagram at a time, a training group would be able to brainstorm a wide range of issues that are likely to impede the communication processes between the three different participants. . . .' (see Figure 4.1) The broken lines between the supervisor and client indicate the indirect relationship and the solid lines the direct relationships present.

Eight potential triads of supervisor, supervisee and client across sexual orientation

	Supervisor	Supervisee	Client
1	Heterosexual	Heterosexual	Homosexual
2	Heterosexual	Homosexual	Homosexual
3	Homosexual	Heterosexual	Homosexual
4	Homosexual	Homosexual	Homosexual
5	Heterosexual	Heterosexual	Heterosexual
6	Heterosexual	Homosexual	Heterosexual
7	Homosexual	Heterosexual	Heterosexual
8	Homosexual	Homosexual	Heterosexual

While each of these offers interesting discussion points some are clearly more pertinent than others are. The first three in the table are selected later for elaboration together with potential scenarios. These are all situations where the client is homosexual across the different possibilities for the supervisor and supervisee.

The issues and supervisory tasks previously discussed are now reviewed through chosen supervisory examples. Scenarios are offered for consideration that may highlight some of the issues in this text. A discussion format in an article on this topic (House and Holloway 1992), provides a framework for the material. The scenarios can be interpreted in many ways; there is no one answer but an invitation to generate hypothesis and negotiate some of the dilemmas that there are in supervisory work. Some of the supervisory dialogues offer examples of excellent practice and others are designed to highlight common errors. At times it may be interesting to consider some from the context of being the supervisor of the supervision. Use the scenarios flexibly.

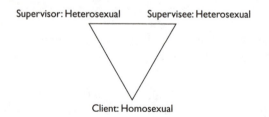

Figure for Scenario 1.1

This is likely to be a common supervisory situation. One of the tasks of the supervisor here, is to facilitate the supervisee in thinking through the various potential issues as previously discussed. The two scenarios below are designed to heighten supervisor awareness and to consider the skills that might be needed.

Scenario 1.1

The supervisee is a religious person. Her religion believes that homosexual people are acceptable in God's eyes as long as they remain celibate. The client in his early twenties is struggling with the possibility of coming to terms with a homosexual identity and has said this in his first session. The supervisee believes that they have already begun making a good relationship and that she can put aside her own religious beliefs in her work.

Dialogue

Supervisee: I really feel for this young man, he really is struggling with his sexuality and I think we are going to work well together.

Supervisor: I can really see that you have energy to work with this client. Have you worked with clients who are struggling with their sexual orientation before?

Supervisee: Yes I've worked with a client in the church counselling service who was similar in many ways – he eventually got married to a young woman he met through the church social club. Also, more recently, a client who has accepted he was homosexual but was struggling to remain celibate.

Supervisor: Am I correct in understanding that your personal value system is one where you value homosexual people as people but you believe that they need to lead celibate lives?

Supervisee: Well those are my religious beliefs – yes, but I wouldn't impose them on clients I work with – I really feel that I can put them aside.

Issues

To what extent is a supervisee able to bracket personal beliefs? What might you think/feel? What would you do/ask? What are the potential implications for this client? How might you take this dialogue forward?

Case analysis

It is likely that this client will be further damaged by a negative evaluation of homosexuality, no matter how partially accepting this counsellor is. The supervisor needs to instigate a discussion with the supervisee of which presenting problems are likely to cause conflict with the supervisee's religious beliefs. The supervisee seems to know at some level that there is a potential problem here, otherwise she would not have brought it in the first place. This ability of the supervisee needs to be acknowledged by the supervisor and consolidated by a discussion of how 'hidden agendas' leak into the therapeutic frame.

Scenario 1.2

Counsellor has worked for 15 sessions with a 31-year-old successful, single man who teaches at a prestigious public school. He presented with mild panic attacks and evidences a level of mild paranoia in his approach to the world. He has had a number of short-term heterosexual relationships, which have ended because both parties have lost interest. He says that he is to some extent bisexual, but wants to use the counselling sessions to help him be free of homosexual thoughts and to find what is getting in the way of him maintaining a hetero-sexual relationship. The counsellor feels uneasy and stuck with this client.

Dialogue

Supervisee: I really feel uneasy and stuck with this client. While he seems open in the sessions I have this feeling that I need to tread on eggshells with this man and I feel anxious and even confused in the sessions with him.

Supervisor: Do you think that your feelings of confusion and anxiety are more yours or his?

Supervisee: Well I'm not usually confused or embarrassed around relationship and sexuality issues.

Supervisor: So possibly you're picking up on his confusion and embarrassment?

Supervisee: Yes that makes sense to me. I guess I really don't know whether he is a predominantly heterosexual man who has some problem in creating relationships or whether he is predominantly homosexual and wants my help in changing his orientation.

Supervisor: They would be two very different contracts.

Supervisee: As we talk, although I don't know for sure, I think he wants my help to rid him of his homosexual feelings – I'm not sure about taking that on.

Supervisor: You're right not to be sure because, if this is what the client wants, there is an ethical question about whether it is right to treat a condition which is not an illness but rather a societal prejudice. Perhaps in the first instance you can clarify with him what the contract really is.

Supervisee: I feel a bit nervous about doing this but that is what I need to do.

Issues

Here the supervisee's over-sensitivity to the client has probably led to collusion around not openly discussing homosexual issues. Here the gentle but firm approach of the supervisor models the process that will facilitate the supervisee in engaging more openly with the client. In this way the supervisor avoids the possibility of entering into a parallel process with her supervisee. The supervisor is aided in this by being clear about her own values, having an understanding of internalized homophobia and being familiar with the potential ethical issues involved.

On the latter point, many approaches have been used to attempt to 'cure' homosexuality including electric shock deconditioning, surgery and long-term psychoanalysis. The potential damage to the individual and the damage inflicted on homosexual people by its very existence is considerable. The ethical dilemma of 'this is what the client wants' versus this is not 'curable' (and is not an individual but a societal pathology) has to be addressed. Bibliotherapy can be invaluable to such supervisees (and of course clients). A further discussion of these issues is given in Davies and Neal (1996: 37–8) and in the *APA Monitor* (1996).

Case analysis

If the client is seeking a change in sexual orientation then the supervisor in this particular example may need to help educate the supervisee through guided reading and discussion. The supervisor also keeps open the possibility that this client may be bisexual to some degree and the issue of removing homosexual feelings is at least in part a diversion from the more significant issue of a problem with intimacy.

Summary of points from Scenarios 1.1 and 1.2

- Be clear about your values and maintain congruency.
- Maintain awareness of homophobia in self and supervisee.
- Maintain awareness of internalized homophobia in homosexual clients.
- Do not allow sensitivity to become homophobic collusion.
- Find a balance to avoid over-exaggeration/minimization of implications of sexual orientation.

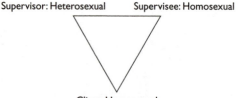

Figure for Scenario 2.1

This supervisory arrangement is likely to be common for those supervisees working in an agency that is set up to provide services for lesbian, gay and bisexual clients or where the supervisee is known as a lesbian/gay counsellor and the client has sought out such a counsellor.

Scenario 2.1

Client, male, 28 years old, has been 'out' for the last three years and has had a number of brief relationships. He has recently met someone but doesn't see the point in pursuing the relationship, as he doesn't believe gay relationships can easily last, are never monogamous and so believes he will end up hurt. He has sought counselling because he cannot bring the relationship to an end and neither can he allow himself to become more emotionally intimate. The supervisee inexplicably feels de-skilled in working with this client.

Dialogue

Supervisee: I feel I don't know where to start with this client because there is a certain degree of truth in some of his beliefs.

Supervisor: Yes obviously there is. Is the new person in his life, one of the promiscuous types of gay man?

Supervisee: I don't think he is particularly.

Supervisor: Maybe your client hasn't really come to terms with his homosexuality and perhaps you should focus on helping him accept the reality of his situation.

Supervisee: Yes maybe you're right – I need to spend more time on his acceptance of his gayness.

Issues

In this dialogue the supervisor shows a homophobic attitude in her statements and assumptions and fails to discuss the supervisee's claim to grains of truth in the client's beliefs. This is an example of exaggerating the significance, in a simplistic way, of the client's homosexuality rather than treating it as valuable context. This essentially closes up the supervisory discussion as to what the issues for the client might be as well as (in this scenario – since the supervisee is designated as homosexual) harming the supervisory relationship.

Case analysis

There is a wide variety of possibilities in this scenario. Leaving the client aside for the moment, the supervisee feels de-skilled because she believes there are grains of truth in the client's belief systems. These were not addressed. In such a scenario it may be that the supervisee is still struggling with the remnants of internalized homophobia herself.

Returning to the client, there are a number of potential issues that could contribute to this client's dilemma. There may be the issues of the want of an idealized relationship; there may be a lack of knowledge of the differences between homosexual and hetero-sexual relationships. There is truth that homosexual relationships are more frequently 'open' although this is usually by negotiation (Kitzinger and Coyle 1995). The belief that 'gay relationships don't last' is clearly homophobic – they can and do. However, the heterosexual model does not have to be mimicked and it may be healthier for a particular individual to have a number of sig-nificant relationships over a lifetime than to remain with one partner.

Scenario 2.2

Counsellor (female) has been working satisfactorily with a female client over the last 12 sessions in which the client has been dealing with the break-up of a two-year lesbian relation-ship. The counsellor reports that she feels very supportive of this client, feels that the work has progressed well and that maybe it's time to stop. The counsellor feels unusually hesitant about bringing up the potential ending with this client and feels confused about why this might be so. She brings this to supervision.

Dialogue

Supervisee: I don't know why but I'm very hesitant to bring up the idea of ending with this client. I have been hoping that maybe she would decide to end but that doesn't seem to be happening.

Supervisor: Do you usually have difficulty ending with clients?

Supervisee: No, this is not usually a problem for me.

Supervisor: What is there about this particular client that might be creating this difficulty.

Supervisee: Nothing that I can think of.

Supervisor: Well maybe if you bring the idea into discussion with your client the difficulty may emerge.

Issue

Here the supervisor has asked some facilitating questions but fails towards the end to explore the common sexuality of both super-visee and client. Out of over-sensitivity, or embarrassment the supervision has not enlarged the supervisee's awareness as much as it could have done.

Case analysis

A possibility here is that there is an erotic transference and perhaps a countertransference happening, which the supervisor needs to feel free to ask about. Not asking might well reinforce in a subtle way a shaming about such feelings and the possibility of increased strengthening of the supervisory relationship is lost. This may also parallel the process between the supervisee and client.

Summary of points from Scenarios 2.1 and 2.2

- Be aware of potential collusion between supervisee and client due to unresolved internalized homophobia.
- Watch for over-sensitivity on the part of supervisor leading to unexplored issues in the supervisory session.
- Be open to the possibility of erotic transference/countertransference impeding the work.
- Understand that the supervisee might withhold information in order to protect self or the client from real or imagined homophobic attitudes on the part of the supervisor.

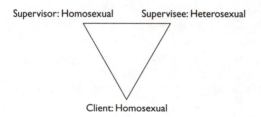

Figure for Scenario 3.1

This arrangement may happen by chance, but it is a valuable supervisory arrangement if the counsellor feels the need of confidence-building about working in this area. The scenarios here, although depicted as set between a homosexual supervisor (with a heterosexual supervisee and homosexual client) are also equally applicable to a knowledgeable heterosexual supervisor.

Scenario 3.1

A young Asian man has presented for counselling and it has emerged in the second session that his distress is about having recently had an arranged marriage. He is happy with his wife and feels very fond of her, but the whole family know 'that he hasn't been a full husband' yet. He wants the counsellor to help him with this. He has had full medical examinations and he has no medical problems. He also adds that he did some years ago have homosexual sex, 'but I stopped that as it wasn't the right way to be'. The counsellor experiences himself in an ethical dilemma since he doubts that the contract wanted by the client is achievable.

Dialogue

Supervisee: Having now told you the outline of this client's situation, I just don't know where to start with this client. I feel for his new wife and the terrible shame he is experiencing in his family. There just doesn't seem to be a way forward. Really I think I should encourage him to get divorced — at least she will have a chance of a proper married life and he could choose to become gay.

Supervisor: It sounds like you feel quite panicked here. Maybe that's how he feels. We have to try to hold the cultural frame here and consider that as context. Perhaps it is not surprising that he would be reluctant to label himself or maybe ever identify as gay and I'm not sure what her cultural position would be even if she would consider divorce.

Supervisee: Yes I guess I'm projecting myself into the situation and imagining what I would want him to do if I were in her position.

Supervisor: What options does the client consider he has?

Supervisee: Only one — to become a sexually potent heterosexual man and at the moment he's impotent with her. This is the contract he wants with me which also involves changing his sexual orientation. The difficulty is that he doesn't label himself as homosexual although tells me that all his masturbatory fantasies are homosexual in content.

Supervisor: It sounds as though your main concern has shifted now away from wanting him or her to separate — now your main concern is that you do not want to accept the contract as stated by him. I understand and support you in this – is there a contract that you might be willing to work with that would also appeal to him in his situation?

Issues

There are many potential issues here. A major issue is the non-acceptance of a contract to change sexual orientation, as previously discussed (see Scenario 1.2). However, this is also set against individual, family and cultural context where it would be unwise to make any kind of confrontation that might 'nudge' the client in any particular direction. This requires that homophobic and gay affirmative agendas on the part of either supervisee or supervisor be carefully monitored.

Case analysis

This particular case highlights the cultural contextual frame that supervisors need to take into account while at the same time maintaining their own ethical frame. It also exists to serve as a striking example of a situation where supervisors/supervisees may need to maintain the humility of not knowing what is right for a particular individual – difficult at times though this may be.

Scenario 3.2

A gay male couple has presented with one of the parties feeling undervalued in the relationship. They have been together for four years. Partner A does not wish to take his Partner B to the company Christmas function as he says he would feel awkward with his staff present. He also visits his parents but never takes B, explaining that his father is difficult and while they know of the relationship, 'there's no point in shoving it under their noses'. A states that it is only for two days twice a year anyway so doesn't understand why B's making such a fuss. The counsellor feels understanding of A's position and cannot figure out why B feels so strongly about this. Thinking she may be missing something she brings this to supervision.

Dialogue

Supervisee: I find A's position to be realistic but then I have this nagging worry that I might be overlooking something.

Supervisor: You are concerned that maybe you're not able to be empathic with B's view of the situation?

Supervisee: Yes that's it precisely – I'm bothered that I'm locked into the same process as goes on between them.

Supervisor: You want my help to facilitate you in looking at both their frames on this issue – OK what would happen if B was for instance black or disabled or belonged to some other such group that is discriminated against – how would this alter your perception?

Supervisee: That's just hit me rather hard – I'm beginning to see how maybe I'm colluding with a subtle degree of homo-phobia. I still feel for A but now I feel more freed up to perhaps help them to understand each other's frame of reference more clearly.

Issues

Without creating shame in the relationship the supervisor finds a way to highlight the homophobic frame that the supervisee out of her awareness, is locked into. Further work on helping the super-visee to recognize her current, marginal positive level of attitude towards homosexuality (see Riddle's scale in Appendix, page 78) would further the developmental direction for this supervisee.

Case analysis

This case offers an excellent example of a couple in which one is at a later stage in the 'coming out' process than the other. Facilitation so that each can perceive the position of the other is likely to lead to some resolution. It is essential in such work that the counsellor has a high awareness of the operation of internalized homophobia and is not seduced by seemingly 'reasonable' arguments.

Summary of points from Scenarios 3.1 and 3.2

- Be alert to counsellor agendas (and your own), both homo-phobic and overly gay affirmative.

- Be alert to differences in the phases of the 'coming out' process as a potential area of conflict.
- Help supervisee develop an awareness of internalized homophobia without shaming.
- Help supervisee think through the complex issues of the interplay between different cultures and gay affirmative psychology.

Summary

The profession of counselling is in a unique position to help end the discrimination against lesbian, gay and bisexual people. We all have the remnants of our early cultural assumptions within us and they are often institutionalized into our society. By developing honest, non-blaming, non-shaming supervisory relationships we can make a contribution to our own development, that of our supervisees and of course their clients.

Training issues

In the training of supervisors to work with this client group, all of the material relevant to the training of counsellors has a place. References to this material have been made throughout the text. In addition to this, trainee supervisors need to develop and maintain an awareness that we tend to look at the world through our given cultural filter which contains heterosexist, sexist, racist, homophobic and ageist assumptions. Usually training in one of these 'cross-cultural' issues will help develop awareness of others. The trainee supervisor also needs to know what to do with such developed awareness. On this point Milton (1997 personal communication) stresses that there is a general agreement about many of the issues involved in working with lesbian, gay and bisexual clients but what is essentially missing is the 'How to' within the supervisory relationship. In summary, supervisor training needs to combine the development of such awareness together with practical supervisory skills. The following are suggested as some training approaches that might be incorporated into training programmes.

- Role-play, perhaps with scenarios derived from the eight potential combinations in the triads as suggested by Lago and Thompson (1997) (see Figure 4.1, page 65).
- Self-assessment exercises – such as Riddle's (1997) four levels of homophobia and four levels of acceptance (see Appendix, below).
- Awareness of models and practices within counselling – ask trainees to actively assess theories and practices for bias from a 'cross-cultural perspective'. For example, from a sexual orientation perspective, trainees might recognize issues such as the inclusion of 'marital status' on assessment forms, to the heterosexist assumptions of models of child development.

Resources

Association for Lesbian, Gay and Bisexual Psychologies – UK (ALGBP – UK)
PO Box 27005
London N2 0WT

This organization is linked to a Europe-wide organization (ALGP – Europe). It aims to support the development of gay affirmative psychology and provide training and referral to gay affirmative therapists. There is an annual conference and occasional workshops are offered.

Appendix

Riddle (1997) homophobia scale lesbian/gay/bisexual identity

Below are listed four negative homophobic levels and four positive levels of attitudes towards lesbian and gay relationships/ people. They were developed by Dr Dorothy Riddle, a psychologist from Arizona, USA.

Homophobic levels of attitude

1. Repulsion: Homosexuality is seen as a 'crime against nature'. Gays/lesbians are sick, crazy, immoral, sinful, wicked, etc. Anything is justified to change them: prison, hospitalization, negative behaviour therapy, electroshock therapy, etc.

2. Pity: Heterosexual chauvinism. Heterosexuality is more mature and certainly to be preferred. Any possibility of 'becoming straight' should be reinforced, and those who seem to be born 'that way' should be pitied, 'the poor dears'.

3. Tolerance: Homosexuality is just a phase of adolescent development that many people go through and most people 'grow out of'. Thus, lesbians/gays are less mature than 'straights' and should be treated with the protectiveness and indulgence one uses with a child. Lesbians/gays should not be given positions of authority because they are still working through their adolescent behaviour.

4. Acceptance: Still implies there is something to accept. Characterized by such statements as 'You're not a lesbian to me, you're a person!' or 'What you do in bed is your own business,' or 'That's fine with me as long as you don't flaunt it!'

Positive levels of attitudes

1. Support: The basic ACLU position. Work to safeguard the rights of lesbians and gays. People at this level may be uncomfortable themselves, but they are aware of the homophobic climate and the irrational unfairness.

2. Admiration: Acknowledges that being lesbian/gay in our society takes strength. People at this level are willing to truly examine their homophobic attitudes, values and behaviours.

3. Appreciation: Value the diversity of people and see lesbians/gays as a valid part of that diversity. These people are willing to combat homophobia in themselves and others.

4. Nurturance: Assumes that gay/lesbian people are indispensable in our society. They view lesbians/gays with genuine affection and delight, and are willing to be allies and advocates.

References

American Psychiatric Association (1990) *Diagnostic and Statistical Manual of Mental Disorders*, 3rd edn. Washington, DC: APA.

APA Monitor (1996) (American Psychological Association) 'Can sexual orientation change with therapy?' *http://www.apa.org/monitor/sep96/converta.html*

Beloff, H. (1993) 'Progress on the BPS Psychology of Lesbianism Front,' *Feminism and Psychology*, 3 (2): 282–3.

Blumenfeld, W.J. and Raymond, D. (1988) *Looking at Gay and Lesbian Life*. Boston: Beacon Press.

Brown, M.T. and Landrum-Brown, J. (1996) 'Counselor supervision: cross-cultural perspectives', in J.G. Ponterotto, J.M. Casas, L.A. Suzuki and C.M. Alexander (eds) *Handbook of Multicultural Counseling*. Thousand Oaks: Sage.

CLGC (Committee on Lesbian and Gay Concerns) (1986) *APA Policy Statement on Lesbian and Gay Issues*. Washington, DC: American Psychological Association.

Cohen, C. and Stein, T. (1986) 'Reconceptualizing individual psychotherapy with gay men and lesbians', in C. Cohen and T. Stein (eds) *Psychotherapy with Lesbians and Gay men*. New York: Plenum Publishing Corp.

Coleman, E. (1985) 'Developmental stages of the coming out process', in J.C. Gonsoriek (ed.) *A Guide to Psychotherapy with Gay and Lesbian Clients*, New York/London: Harrington Park.

Coyle, A., Kitzinger, C., Flynn, R., Wilkinson, S., Rivers, I. and Perkins, R. (1995) 'Lesbian and Gay Psychology Section' (correspondence), *The Psychologist*, 8 (4): 151.

Davies, D. (1996) 'Towards a model of gay affirmative therapy', in D. Davies and C. Neal (eds) *Pink Therapy – A Guide for Counsellors and Therapists Working with Lesbian, Gay and Bisexual Clients*. Buckingham/Philadelphia: Open University Press.

Davies, D. and Neal, C. (1996) *Pink Therapy – A Guide for Counsellors and Therapists Working with Lesbian, Gay and Bisexual Clients*. Buckingham/Philadelphia: Open University Press.

Ellis, M.L. (1994) 'Lesbians, gay men and psychoanalytic training', *Free Associations: Psychoanalysis, Groups, Politics*, 4 (32): 501–17.

Garnets, L. and Kimmel, D. (1991) 'Lesbian and gay male dimensions in the psychological study of human diversity', in J. Goodchilds (ed.) *Psychological Perspectives in Human Diversity in America: Masters Lectures*. Washington, DC: American Psychological Association.

Gebhard, P.H. (1972) 'Incidence of overt homosexuality in the United States and Western Europe', in J.J. Livingood (ed.) *NIMH Task Force on Homosexuality: Final Report and Background Papers*. DHEW publication no. (HSM) 72–9116. Rockville, MD: National Institute of Mental Health.

Gonsiorek, J.C. (ed.) (1985) *A Guide to Psychotherapy with Gay and Lesbian Clients*. New York: Harrington Park.

Gramick, J. (1983) 'Homophobia: a new challenge', *Social Work*, 28 (2): 137–41.

Greene, B. (1994) 'Ethnic minority lesbian and gay men: mental health and treatment issues', *Journal of Consulting and Clinical Psychology*, 62 (2): 243–51.

Hanley-Hackenbruck, P. (1989) 'Psychotherapy and the "Coming out process" ', *Journal of Gay and Lesbian Psychotherapy*, 1 (1): 21–40.

Harry, J. (1983) 'Gay male and lesbian relationships', in E. Macklin and R. Rubin (eds) *Contemporary Families and Alternative Lifestyles: Handbook on Research and Theory*. London: Sage.

Herek, G.M. (1991) 'Stigma, prejudice and violence against lesbians and gay men', in J.C. Gonsiorek and J.D. Weinrich (eds) *Homosexuality: Research Implications for Public Policy*. Newbury Park, CA: Sage.

Hitchings, P. (1997) 'Counselling and sexual orientation', in S. Palmer and G.

McMahon (eds) *Handbook of Counselling* (2nd edn). London and New York: Routledge.

House, R.M. and Holloway, E.L. (1992) 'Empowering the counseling professional to work with gay and lesbian issues', in S.H. Dworkin and F.J. Gutierrez (eds) *Counselling Gay Men and Lesbians: Journey to the End of the Rainbow*. Alexandria, VA: American Association for Counseling and Development.

Hudson, W.W. and Ricketts, W.A. (1980) 'A strategy for the measurement of homophobia', *Journal of Homosexuality*, 5 (4): 317–72.

Kinsey, A., Pomeroy, W. and Martin, C. (1948) *Sexual Behavior in the Human Male*. Philadelphia: Saunders.

Kitzinger, C. and Coyle, A. (1995) 'Lesbian and gay couples: speaking of difference', *The Psychologist*, 8 (2): 64–9.

Kowszun, G. and Malley, M. (1996) 'Alcohol and substance misuse', in D. Davies and C. Neal (eds) *Pink Therapy – A Guide for Counsellors and Therapists Working with Lesbian, Gay and Bisexual Clients*. Buckingham/Philadelphia: Open University Press.

Krajeski, J.P. (1986) 'Psychotherapy with gay men and lesbians: a history of controversy', in T.S. Stein and C.J. Cohen (eds) *Contemporary Perspectives on Psychotherapy with Lesbians and Gay Men*. New York: Plenum.

Lago, C. and Thompson, J. (1997) 'The triangle with curved sides: sensitivity to issues of race and culture in supervision', in G. Shipton (ed.) *Supervision of Psychotherapy and Counselling – Making a Place to Think*. Buckingham: Open University Press.

Marsella, A. and Pedersen, P. (eds) (1981) *Cross Cultural Counselling and Psychotherapy*. New York: Pergamon Press.

Maylon, A. (1982) 'Psychotherapeutic implications of internalized homophobia in gay men', in J. Gonsiorek (ed.) *Homosexuality and Psychotherapy*. New York: Haworth Press.

Messing, A.E., Schoenberg, R. and Stephens, R.K. (1984) 'Confronting homophobia in health care settings: guidelines for social work practice', in R. Schoenberg, R.S. Goldberg and D.A. Shore (eds) *Homosexuality and Social Work*. New York: Haworth Press.

Meyer, J.K. (1985) 'Ego-dystonic homosexuality', in H. Kaplan and B. Sadock (eds) *Comprehensive Textbook of Psychiatry IV*. Baltimore, MD: Williams & Wilkins.

Milton, M. (1997) personal communication, University of Surrey.

Morin, S. (1977) 'Heterosexual bias in psychological research on lesbianism and male homosexuality', *American Psychologist*, 32: 629–37.

Morin, S. and Rothblum, E. (1991) 'Removing the stigma: fifteen years of progress', *American Psychologist*, 46: 947–9.

Moses, A. and Hawkins, R. (1982) 'Counselling lesbian women and gay men: a life-issues approach', St Louis, MO: Mosby.

The Psychologist (1995) 8 (3) (April): 'Letters'.

Rabin, J., Keefe, K. and Burton, M. (1986) 'Enhancing services to sexual minority clients: a community mental health approach', *Social Work*, 31 (4): 294–8.

Remafedi, G., Farrow, J.A. and Deisher, R.W. (1991) 'Risk factors for attempted suicide in gay and bisexual youth', *Paediatrics*, 87 (6), 869–75.

Riddle, D. (1997) 'Riddle homophobia scale' at *http://www.wiu.edu/users/mitfeh/riddle.htm*

Samuels, A. (1995) 'Letter for Publication' in *Dramatherapy*, Summer: 47–53.

—————— (1997) Unpublished keynote address to British Association for Supervision Practice and Research Conference in London.

Sell, R.L., Wells, J.A., Valleron, A.J., Will, A., Cohen, M. and Umbel, K. (1990) 'Homosexual and bisexual behavior in the United States, the United Kingdom and France'. Paper presented at the Sixth International Conference on AIDS, San Francisco, CA, June.

Shidlo, A. (1994) 'Internalized homophobia – conceptual and empirical issues in measurement', in B. Greene and G.M. Herek (eds) *Psychological Perspectives on Lesbian and Gay Issues: Vol. 1. Lesbian and Gay Psychology – Theory, Research and Clinical Applications*. Thousand Oaks, CA: Sage.

Simon, G. (1996) 'Working with people in relationships', in D. Davies and C. Neal (eds) *Pink Therapy – A Guide for Counsellors and Therapists Working with Lesbian, Gay and Bisexual Clients*. Buckingham/Philadelphia: Open University Press.

Thompson, J. (1991) 'Issues of race and culture in counselling supervision training courses', unpublished MSc dissertation, Polytechnic of East London.

Tievsky, D.L. (1988) 'Homosexual clients and homophobic social workers', *Journal of Independent Work*, 2 (3): 51–62.

Weinberg, G. (1972) *Society and the Healthy Homosexual*. New York: St Martin's Press.

Woodman, N.J. and Lenna, H.R. (1980) *Counselling with Gay Men and Women: A Guide for Facilitating Positive Lifestyles*. San Francisco, CA: Jossey Bass.

II Supervision and organizational issues

accept these limits cannot support the counsellor to wrestle positively with the implications of them.

The range of clients is greater in general practice than in private practice. Counsellors must expect to work with more differences in social class, culture, race, income, employment status, and psychiatric history than is common in other settings. Women are more likely to seek counselling than men – typically approximately 70 per cent women to 30 per cent men (Speirs and Jewell 1995; Cambridgeshire FHSA figures 1993; Henderson 1995).

The GP may particularly want help with patients who have multiple social problems, some of whom also have the thick files which characterize the high utilizers often called 'heartsink patients'. As Social Services can offer less help with these patients because of their own funding pressures and priorities, the GPs have turned to counsellors to include them in their client load. Since this definition refers to the GP's heart that sinks as they enter, it signals some questions about the referral process: Why is this patient being referred? why now? and why to me? Mathers et al. (1995) report that 60 per cent of the variance in the number of heartsink patients that GPs reported on their lists could be accounted for by four characteristics of the GPs: greater perceived workload, lower job satisfaction, lack of training in counselling and/or communication skills, and lack of appropriate postgraduate qualifications. They note that such labelling allows the GP to avoid confronting their own negative emotions about patients who make high demands on them. Unless the supervisor is interested in helping the counsellor to understand the meaning and structures of the triangular relationships of referral, they should avoid general practice.

Approximately 70 per cent of consultations with GPs entail symptoms without a primarily bio-medical explanation; and a very small percentage of these is referred for counselling. Few counsellors, therefore, believe that they get referrals which are inappropriate, just that there are more who could come than there is time to work with. Among those patients who 'somatize' their distress, some may be convinced that something medical is wrong with them. Some accept that life circumstances and emotions are creating or contributing to physical symptoms, but use the symptom as a ticket of entry to the GP. They may have undergone a large number of medical checks or interventions before being referred to the counsellor. Counsellors and their supervisors in general practice can usefully be curious about mind–body connections and refer to those models of health and illness which seek meaning for symptoms. These may focus on triggers to stress and anxiety, family relationships, cultural attitudes to particular illnesses, and to the stigma some of these carry, as well as the emotional consequences of being diagnosed with chronic or terminal illness. Counsellors could work routinely with patients with heart conditions, diabetes and asthma, as they do in the USA, but these are seldom referred to UK counsellors in general practice.

Counsellor characteristics in general practice

The counsellor needs to be trained and experienced enough to assess and create a plan to work in a focused way with clients who bring a variety of emotional issues, and then to follow it through within the relationships between the counsellor, client and the GP (Berkowitz 1996). Trainees are only appropriately placed in general practice if there is a counsellor on site to provide mentoring – possibly even initial screening and allocation of suitable clients only – or if they have frequent (weekly) supervision from a supervisor with experience of counselling in general practice. Ideally, counsellors should be experienced enough to be accreditable, and clear enough about the gaps in their expertise to refuse inappropriate referrals and seek further training before they offer counselling about issues arising in the patient population of the practice which are new to them. If the counsellor seeks supervision about elements new to the supervisor it is important that the supervisor is clear too about the limits to his or her own expertise. Burton et al. (1998) found that in their sample of 90 counsellors in general practice, 92 per cent were female, and they were fairly, but not very, experienced – the mean years of supervised counselling in the sample was 7 (range 1–18 years). Most were not accredited with either the British Association for Counselling (BAC) or the United Kingdom Council for Psychotherapy (UKCP). Kendrick et al. (1993) found many more who did not have a counselling Diploma working within the role in general practice, some combining it with other roles such as CPN or practice nurse on the basis of a Certificate in Counselling in addition to their other experience and qualifications. Typically, counsellors in general practice come from three sources: NHS and Social Services staff, counsellors from Relate, or those from private practice with no experience of the setting prior to their appointment.

Training for counsellors

A course for counsellors who wish to work, or are working in general practice thus needs five components to fulfil the complex roles in this setting:

- Significant opportunities for personal and professional development, particularly to come to grips with ethical issues around confidentiality, and any issues in their personal history about doctors and the practice of medicine, and to reflect on and develop their capacity to work with differences (of race, culture, class, gender, age, sexuality, and so on).
- Exploration of multi-disciplinary teamwork, both to understand the current structures and culture of the NHS, and to develop the skills of collaborative work, building trust, agreeing structures for answerability and appropriate contracts and developing the communication skills necessary to give an account of their work to colleagues from other professions. Thinking about audit and evaluation, and developing basic skills to undertake their own is essential in this regard.
- Models of health and illness, exploration of attitudes to medication for mental illness and some understanding about it. Awareness of the mind–body links, and some of the ways people express emotional distress through physical symptoms is helpful.
- Development of understanding and skill in time-limited therapy.
- Identification of any gaps in initial and subsequent training which need to be addressed on the course, or later. For example, it is common to learn the basics of bereavement counselling on a Certificate or a Diploma course; it may be less common to have addressed the complicated grief arising from suicide, murder, sudden death: or avoided grief and some of its physical manifestations.

These ideas emerged initially from research with counsellors working in general practice who reflected on the gaps in their initial training in preparing them for work in this setting (Einzig et al. 1995). Clearly supervisors also need to be confident about these issues.

Counsellors in general practice need to be comfortable in working with adults who were sexually abused as children, about eating disorders, relationship issues and breakdown, and when depression is susceptible to counselling. They must have a capacity to help clients who come seeking assistance with anxiety and panic. Teaching counsellors to work in general practice is not simply a matter of a cognitive focus. The primary aim is to support the development of more reflective practitioners (Schon 1987) able to engage in internal supervision while they are with clients and after they have seen them (Casement 1985). An essential element of professional development is that the counsellor is open to other views while able to assert the value of and explain their own. *Development of their capacity to give an account of their work that is sufficiently coherent that other professionals can understand and work alongside with mutual respect is vital.*

The general practice context: client load and contact

The context refers to the numbers of clients held in a caseload by these counsellors, the management of waiting lists, referral processes and relationships within the practice and with other providers of psychological services.

Caseloads in general practice are generally high, and many patients are 'held' by the counsellor over a long period, paralleling the GP role in terms of continuity of care. There is an issue here for the pattern of contracts offered to counsellors in the UK, which are too often renewed, if at all, on an annual basis, which may seriously undermine this continuity of care from the counsellor. Burton et al. (1998) found in their sample that caseloads open at any one time were reported as being between 3 and 65 clients, with a mean of 14.5. Since many counsellors are part-time, and some work in more than one practice, many are carrying a heavy load. With an average of 6.8 sessions per client, these counsellors 'hold in mind' a large number of clients in the course of a year. There are implications for supervision, especially when the supervisor and counsellor only meet fortnightly or once a month. In particular, the contract for supervision needs to include review of the emotional resilience of a counsellor working under these conditions, and provide regular space for Inskipp and Proctor's 'restorative function' (1995) while avoiding intrusion which turns supervision into therapy.

Waiting lists build up in many practices: the average wait in the Burton study was 7.1 weeks, the longest was 26 weeks. Inexperienced counsellors in general practice can use supervision to manage it by keeping assessment slots, keeping 'emergency' slots, or doing regular stock takes of their client list. There is a significant shift in thought processes for the counsellor used to private practice, to begin to allocate sessions in the light of needs of those on the waiting list or of the patient population as a whole. Thus all counsellors have to *manage a counselling service*. Supervision can remind them to address these issues, despite the pull from initial training to consider only the needs of those currently in relationship as clients. Many counsellors who have not fully made the transition to this context talk about 'shutting their minds' to the waiting list in order to work effectively with those in front of them. This does not endear them to colleagues in a service whose basic culture requires the other practitioners to see all comers, nor is it necessarily more morally desirable in terms of answerability to the patient population as a whole. All parties have to address the realities of working within a service under pressure, like a volcano building up, and not wait for the crisis to erupt to address issues about the service planning as a whole.

With this level of turnover of clients, many may never be brought to supervision, especially by experienced counsellors. It is good practice for the counsellor to bring a list of current clients at agreed intervals, so that the counsellor and supervisor can identify those who have never been discussed in supervision. In my experience this encourages the counsellor to do her own internal audit, reflection, and preparation for supervision, and thus to identify which clients or issues she brings and which she does not. More contentious is the supervisory issue about clients who wish to continue to see the counsellor in a private capacity after they have completed the allocated sessions within the practice. Some supervisors take a rigid line, that such alterations to the contract can never be managed well in the client's interest. Others accept it is possible, but caution that both the GP and the supervisor need to be consulted before an individual change is agreed. It may depend on the pragmatics of the practice population and the balance of needs and capacity to pay.

The multi-disciplinary team

The counsellor in general practice works within a multi-disciplinary team in which the dominant culture has very different assumptions about how to intervene, and sometimes a completely different explanatory model about what ails people and how best to treat them. There may be little *teamwork*: often the GPs may actually work as a disparate set of individuals. Issues will arise about the nature of the responsibility of both the counsellor and the supervisor. Conflicts of loyalty are endemic to the role of counsellor. Different definitions and perceptions of responsibility may be held by the supervisor, the counsellor, the referring GP, and possibly other NHS or Social Services staff involved with a client, and these are exacerbated when each one comes from a different profession. The contractual element of these responsibilities needs to be spelled out, and the moral responsibilities which arise from relationships with patients and their GPs raise questions of answerability which can usefully be explored and clarified.

The counsellor also needs to build a capacity to liaise appropriately with each GP in the practice, and with the health visitor and nurse colleagues, and members of the community mental health team. They have to be able to speak the language of diagnostic categories used by these colleagues, and be able to give an account of their work without the counselling jargon becoming an impenetrable barrier to multi-disciplinary understanding; ideally they need a working knowledge of some basics of psycho-pharmacology.

There are complexities arising from roles and relationships. Counsellors frequently fall into informal caring roles for colleagues in the practice. On occasion they offer a formal counselling contract to colleagues, usually of a limited nature around a life crisis. Management of the colleague role then needs careful and sensitive attention. This is particularly so when informal counselling for stress, bereavement, relationship breakdown or difficulty with a patient has been offered to the GP who later has to exercise authority in their position of employer to the counsellor. The ethical issues of managing collaborative work while sustaining appropriate confidentiality tax both counsellor and supervisor at times.

Supervision issues about collaborative work in the multi-disciplinary team are usually about referral, relationships and liaison, and the management of confidentiality within the team. Supervision about the referral process is useful, and needs to be a normal part of the clinical work. This includes referral *to* the counsellor, as indicated above, and also referral *back* to the GP or *on* to other providers. Berkowitz (1996) explores assessment in detail and makes useful comments about shared care with the GP. Woodhouse and Pengelly (1991), in a useful text, describe from a psychoanalytic viewpoint the triangle of referral (p. 67), collaborative triangles (pp. 58–9), parallel process in referrals (p. 43) and the misuse of agency and professional boundaries for purposes of institutional defence (p. 8). Theirs is a text which stimulates thought about collaboration and the context of work with medical colleagues, and can usefully be read by supervisors who lack a background in organizational consultation or who are interested in a psychoanalytic view of it. Effective multi-disciplinary team-work relies on the development of trust between members. This is built by informal and formal meetings between the counsellor and members of the practice staff, but these are rare in many practices. Liaison and confidentiality within a team has to be negotiated, and the supervisor has to be briefed on how the counsellor is building effective relationships of trust with each GP if, as usual, there is no direct contact between the supervisor and the GPs. Writing about trust and partnership in schools, Nias (1996) argues that to share responsibility is to share control; she notes that a common impulse is to retain control over activities for which people see themselves as answerable. Unclear divisions of labour cause problems here, while improved communication, clearer explanations of intentions or policies build trust. She usefully identifies three obstacles to partnership in schools which in my view also apply to this context.

1. Fear of losing control especially over deciding aims, priorities and the form of a service. (In general practice this includes the reality that GPs retain clinical responsibility for the patients.)
2. The lengthy and time-consuming nature of negotiation to develop a shared language. (The pace of work in the NHS is legendary.)
3. The human cost of negotiation which requires the time and energy to fit it in, and the willingness and effort to see the issues through the eyes of those who may differ profoundly with you.

Nias talks of 'Balkanised cultures and turf wars', which arise when conflicts are not addressed, and reminds us that collaboration requires all parties to work at it. Meetings do promote such links to develop sufficient shared values and mutual trust. In a busy general practice this can take years to develop. One description by a counsellor of a Practice barbecue shows how an acute observer notices relationships even when relaxing, and is affected by seeing colleagues out of formal roles:

> C: The barbecue last week turned around a lot of feelings for me. I met nurses, physio, cleaner; I heard terrible disrespect by receptionists. GPs were there, lots with children under 5. There was a rounders match. I've never seen such competition in my life! It's as if there's this hidden agenda in the practice, as if the receptionists are in a quite powerful position; and the banter. . . . One GP was trying to arrange a meeting with the nurses. She was working, the others were sitting around. The cleaner was very dominant. He ended up bowling and taking charge. The senior GP emerged as quite shy. More of a scapegoat. I think he's quite isolated and makes some hard decisions by himself. I feel very sympathetic to him.
>
> S: What I hear is almost a soft affection in your voice. As a result of participating, you can let go of some of your projections.
>
> C: The young GP was the biggest shock. I knew then – after seeing him play rounders – that he *was* a force to be reckoned with!

Supervision can keep the issue of collaboration alive for the counsellor and help a counsellor to keep working to improve relationships even under less than ideal conditions.

Brief counselling

Supervision of brief therapy, especially about assessment and agreements and challenges of work within a contract, tends to be the bread and butter of the clinical element of this supervision. Many counsellors have not been taught assessment skills, and they are necessary. Person-centred counsellors have relatively recently come to their own way to incorporate this in their model (Mearns 1994); psychodynamic counsellors have been prolific in reflecting on it with varying degrees of flexibility in applying their theoretical frame (Hoag 1992; Jones et al. 1994; Lees 1997), though their view of what constitutes a brief contact may be up to 20 sessions rather than up to 6. Whatever the theoretical base, the counsellor needs tools and skills for agreeing a focus for brief work with a client, or their intervention may not fit what the setting (or the patient) requires of them. Gilbert and Shmukler (1996: 187–96) usefully explore contracts and the supervision of them, and remind readers of the need to learn how to design 'homework' assignments, and of the central importance of addressing issues of power in supervision of brief counselling.

Supervisors may discuss the use of time by the counsellor who may vary session lengths, offering shorter or longer than standard sessions for initial assessment, according to her theoretical base; she may alter the frequency of meetings from weekly to fortnightly to monthly. She will have to develop a policy with the GPs about DNAs (shorthand for 'did not attend').

Supervisors may discuss the use of the relationship by the counsellor. Whatever the theoretical approach to brief counselling, the counsellor must be capable of creating rapport and a working alliance within the first session or two. She has to develop her capacity to work deeply while making choices in interventions which reduce or avoid the creation of dependency. Daniel Stern, an American psychiatrist talked in his John Bowlby Memorial Lecture in London in March 1997 of 'moments of meeting' in therapy, those occasions when genuineness and immediacy (my terms for his ideas) pervade the exchange, and something transformative happens to create an intimacy and sense of connection for both client and therapist, and enables the client to move on from where they are stuck.

The match of supervisor–supervisee frames of thought is important, and lack of it can sometimes be very difficult if a counsellor is allocated to a supervisor she would not freely choose. In the study by Burton et al. (1998), 87 per cent of respondents did have a choice; 89 per cent noted a good match between their theoretical frame and their supervisor's; and 96 per cent noted there was a good match of personal style with their supervisor. Comments they made in reply to the question signal some of the ease and the difficulty that can occur in difference:

> I'm moving away from psychodynamic work, utilizing systems and brief therapy models more. Often we are learning together about these models. She is still very helpful, but it's often more of a peer relationship.

My clinical supervisor has recently done further training in brief therapy as she is aware her training is in long-term therapy. I feel she understands the problems of transference in brief therapy and has helped me with this.

Sometimes I feel I cannot follow any direct advice that is given because it does not fit my training. Also we have different attitudes to clients and therapy generally at times. (Supervisor is a clinical psychologist)

Solution-focus ideas have become popular in the UK in recent years, largely because they are client-centred though very focused, and are distinctive for their emphasis on conveying optimism and hope of making life changes (for example Jane Lethem 1994; or Insoo Kim Berg 1994). They share roots in the narrative methods popularized by Epston and White (1990). These ideas about making meaning through creating coherent narratives, less problem-saturated narratives, and exploring symptoms and addictions by 'externalizing the problem' (for example, how can you overcome your symptom? when does it beat you?) can be very useful to the counsellor in general practice. O'Connell and Jones's useful article (1997) brings references from the journal of systemic therapies to the supervision of solution-focused counselling, and emphasizes the parallel processes in supervision: interest in language, seeking exceptions to the problem – that is, noticing when things are going right. Humanistic counsellors use methods such as exploring and using metaphors, working in the here and now and so on. Most counsellors who are experienced work within more than one theoretical frame. I was struck by the degree to which Lees (1997) who describes work in a very economically deprived area from a psychodynamic base, also uses interventions which emphasize hope and client's strengths.

Supervisors' roles and skills in general practice

The role and tasks of supervisors in this setting are complex, and their approach may well be affected by their professional background. Burton et al. (1998) found in their sample a total of 51 per cent of supervisors of counsellors in general practice who were not themselves counsellors (22 per cent were psychotherapists, 18 per cent were counselling or clinical psychologists, 8 per cent were social workers and 3 per cent were psychiatrists). It would be useful to identify the consequences for counsellors' supervision of these different professional approaches.

In many Health Trusts, counselling in general practice is part of managed psychological services. Here the supervisor may be a clinical psychologist, member of the Community Mental Health Team, or even a psychiatrist. Where scarce resources result in professional rivalries over access to clients or to money, supervisors may be involved in conflicts of loyalty on their own behalf. Other problems of supervision in general practice are more likely to arise because the supervisor has no direct experience of the setting. Burton et al. noted that 75 per cent of supervisors in their sample were not known to any GP in the practice, and only 25 per cent worked clinically in general practice.

Fitzgerald and Murphy (1997) describe the Derbyshire FHSA initiatives to train counsellors in general practice. They note the value of a mentor in addition to a clinical supervisor, and describe the organizational structures they've developed to enhance efficacy in the counsellor. Curtis Jenkins et al. (1997) build on these ideas to propose four distinct roles which may usefully be offered by different people: the mentor, the clinical supervisor, the multi-professional consultancy group and the manager. He urges supervisors to ensure someone is responsible for each role. In the same publication, Henderson explores the importance of attending to context in supervision of counselling in general practice, Foster identifies useful elements of the supervisor–supervisee contract; and Inskipp outlines ideas for training. Henderson highlights the supervisor's role as a linguistic interpreter between the medical and counselling models, and the necessity to take an interest in systemic issues about the waiting list, referrals, and relationships with colleagues.

Key elements of the supervisor's clinical role are to help the counsellor to manage her feelings, to manage professional issues, and to explore transference issues with patients and colleagues. Sometimes the GP or the administration, not always aware of the impact, may affect the counselling with a client by making sudden changes to existing arrangements. Supervision can be a place for a suitably restorative expression of frustration, followed by a systemic analysis of how to proceed. It is crucial that the supervisor is free enough of personal issues about the setting and that he or she retains sufficient objectivity to avoid the temptation to join in and blame the doctors too.

With the Patient's Charter and increasing litigation, fear of complaint can underlie the work in this setting, and some managerial input is useful. Being able to hold and process these feelings in clinical supervision enables the supervisor to support the counsellor to avoid precipitate, anxiety-driven action. It is essential for both the supervisor and the counsellor to have professional liability insurance, and while the GP generally checks that the counsellor is insured, very few would think to ask if the supervisor is, so it behoves the counsellor to do so.

Patients in this setting may transfer expectations to the counsellor from the GP. They are likely to come hoping for cure, and expecting diagnosis, advice, and the power dynamic between expert and compliant (or resistant) lay person. They may expect the GP and counsellor to consult and work together; in one way or another they come because the doctor suggested it. If counsellor and GP see the client together, they demonstrate their capacity to collaborate in her interest. Lees (1997) develops a concept he calls 'ubiquitous transference' to describe the impact of the setting as a whole on the work. A mentor who knows the personalities and the systems can be invaluable in promoting what is possible in collaboration.

Summary

In sum, the unique features of supervision in this setting entail supporting the counsellor to set limits and identify priorities and work briefly some or most of the time; encouraging her to manage the workload, waiting lists and referral process, and pressing her to take seriously the opportunities and requirements for collaboration, even when there is little time and limited opportunity for it. There will be challenges to learn how to work with the huge range of issues clients bring to counselling. Supervision also must attend to the sheer volume and weight of the work required, and the pace of the context.

A major contribution any supervisor makes is to create a space where the counsellor can seek to understand and make meaning of the experiences at work. In the pressurized and busy setting of general practice, an issue is the acknowledgement and management of fear and powerful feelings; this parallels the GP's pressures as they deal with issues of life and death, and the projections on them of omniscience or expertise. For supervision to be useful it is necessary for supervisor and counsellor to respect each other, and ensure both clarity about the methods being used and consistency in the power relationship between client and counsellor across the methods.

Supervision example

The next section of the chapter outlines a case of supervision that illustrates some of the issues unique to the context. I want to note how far the parallel process between the counselling context and the supervision can affect supervision. Counselling in general practice is work in a very pressured and busy environment, within a culture of scarcity. It is easy for the supervision also to get so busy that there is a sense of there being too much to attend to. It is a discipline to create a sense of space for whatever is most useful, which parallels the focus required in brief therapy. The supervisor is required to hold the 'helicopter vision' (Carroll 1996) and keep a weather eye on the perennial issues about boundaries, responsibilities, and the relationships and structures of the context.

Susie Orbach writing in the *Guardian* (1997) made a passionate plea about the dangers of managed services in medical settings. Supervisor and counsellor have to be aware that the GP and other medical colleagues have the right to make final decisions about patient care. It is a challenge for supervisors/counsellors to know their limits while still attending to the implications when others make decisions which seem inimical to client well-being, and yet continue to work at the relationships with colleagues. An example occurred when a counsellor reported work with a student client:

> *Counsellor*: . . . going on to issues of confidentiality. A student seeing me and the GP for psychological and learning behavioural work on dyslexia. He wanted a psychiatric assessment to check out any neurological difficulties. The student got referred privately, the psychiatrist decided he was manic depressive and was going to bung him on Lithium. My reaction was one of horror, and I revealed it to the GP . . . I just felt uneasy on so many levels: (a) That I was talking about it to him at all, (b) that I let my feelings out, and (c) his different position: 'I've seen people do very well on Lithium.' I said: 'But where's the bloody evidence that he's manic?' He's a very experienced psychiatrist, and I felt awkward at showing my prejudice and outrage. I felt he was completely

off the ball-park. Having known the psychopathology of it, I know what's wrong with this kid. There are uncertainties *vis-à-vis* the medical model, and also my embarrassment that I didn't keep cool, calm, and collected as a doctor and a counsellor should. I didn't feel reasonable. I felt bloody outraged – a psychiatrist charging a fortune who sees this guy for five minutes, he's got nothing to lose, and the client was left labelled with what is usually seen as an affective disorder, with a psychosis, and I was left uncomfortable, and I've been uncomfortable with the GP ever since.

Supervisor: I wonder how you can process what happened?

Counsellor: It's very friendly. We chat about his baby, but I've got the feeling he lost confidence in another professional and I feel inarticulate about it.

Supervisor: You are being articulate now. I wonder what happens to you if you feel like you lose your cool and lose your recognition from another professional that what you say is valid – do you see it as a personal or a professional issue?

Counsellor: As a professional and gender issue about rivalry. Rivalrous views of the world, but also my fear is that because he's so powerful in the practice, his view carries sway in the universe I enter when I walk through those doors. I wonder if it is a male gender thing too. . . .

This extract demonstrates the number of choices a supervisor might make about what to address first. To take up the first statement of the counsellor that the issue was about confidentiality; or teamwork and relationship issues, especially around loss of face, or the rivalry between different views of the world, or gender issues, or the moral responsibility to the patient, or the problems of multi-disciplinary work, or the financial rivalry as part of turf wars, and so on. This exchange took place in the counsellor's first six months in the practice, so trust had not been developed sufficiently between counsellor and GP for such a robust exchange. The supervisor and counsellor came back to it on a number of occasions to monitor how the relationship between counsellor and GP had improved since that point.

Training for supervisors

Generic training for supervisors has only recently been developed, and a good summary of the ethical base and a model curriculum is included in Carroll (1996), or available as a self-study pack in Inskipp and Proctor (1995). For this context, the reader will not be surprised to read a recommendation to include the following as essential:

- The development of some understanding about the organiza-tional matters described above.
- Knowledge about the structures and culture of the NHS, and work in a medical setting, with colleagues from other pro-fessions.
- Continuing training and development of the supervisor's own capacity for and understanding of working with difference.
- Ability to help counsellors with difficult issues of assessment, and a working knowledge of the DSM V categories of mental illness used by medical professions.
- Some understanding of brief therapy, and how to apply it and when it is not appropriate for this clientele.
- The requirements of the setting for record keeping and admin-istration, and a working knowledge of basic audit skills.
- Ideally, a grasp of group work, if the counsellors seeking supervision are considering offering groups either with health visitors or on their own.

This list relates closely to Inskipp (in Curtis Jenkins et al. 1997), who articulated the ideas on behalf of a group of experienced supervisors who met to debate the implications for training of Burton et al.'s research in 1996.

As an example, my preoccupation with persuading the reader of the importance of grasping the organizational element of supervision in general practice led me to organize a discussion in a training session to explore the moral and contextual dilemmas. Members paired to explore one set of the questions from the following list which were of most relevance to their own practice. Each pair then taught another pair the key issues they'd identi-fied. The group then fed back key learning under four general headings.

As supervisor of a counsellor in general practice, discuss with your partner any two of the following questions:

1. *Roles and relationships*: In what ways does the counsellor feel part of the organizational team? Can you list their formal

and informal roles in the organization? When do these roles conflict? Do you discuss relationships with others in the team in supervision? Is the supervisor aware of the culture of the organization? Are you able to describe both it, and its impact on the expectations of clients and referrers?

2. *Accountability*: To whom does the counsellor *feel* accountable for the work? How does this match with formal accountability? How do you manage conflicts of loyalty?

3. *Assessment*: How far does supervision help with assessing client's suitability for short-term therapy? or to say no to an unsuitable client? Is the work subject to arbitrary limits (e.g. six-session maximum)? If the counsellor is unhappy about this for a client, does supervision help to tackle it with the referrer in the organization?

4. *Referrals*: Do you attend to systemic issues and triangular relationships? Does the supervisor help to reflect on the meaning of referrals to the counsellor? How has the supervisor helped the counsellor to pass referrals on to others? Do you reflect on the meaning of referrals: Why now? Why to the counsellor? What does this signal about the referrer's view of the counsellor? Do you reflect on split transferences? (That is, do people come to see the counsellor because of strong feelings they have, positive or negative, about the person referring them or the organization itself?)

In my concluding comments I want to come back to the unique supervisory focus which results from the ideas in this chapter. I believe it is essential to offer some stillness in supervision, or at least some slowing down, to create space for reflection and creativity from a frenetic context. I argue for including rigorous review of the contextual elements. I assert the value of supporting counsellors to continue to develop and review their approach, to capitalize on the opportunities that counselling work in this setting provides, and to do the same with relationships with colleagues which are an essential basis for collaborative continuing care of the clients. Most particularly I would encourage supervisors to explore with supervisees what they are answerable for and to whom, and how they will keep these issues in the forefront of their attention.

References

Berg, I.K. (1994) *Family Preservation – A Brief Therapy Workbook*, London: Brief Therapy Press.

Berkowitz, R. (1996) 'Assessment: some issues for counsellors in primary health care', *Psychodynamic Counselling*, 2 (2): 209–29.

Burton, M., Henderson, P. and Curtis Jenkins, G. (1998) *Primary Care Counsellors' Experiences of Supervision Counselling*, 9 (2): 122. London: Counselling in Primary Care Trust.

Carroll, M. (1996) *Counselling Supervision: Theory, Skills and Practice*, London: Cassell.

Casement, P. (1985) *On Learning from the Patient*, London: Tavistock.

Curtis Jenkins, G., Burton, M., Henderson, P., Foster, J. and Inskipp, F. (1997) 'Supplement no. 3 on supervision of counsellors in primary care' (including papers by Curtis Jenkins, Henderson, Foster and Inskipp), available free from the Counselling in Primary Care Trust, Majestic House, High Street, Staines TW18 4DG.

Einzig, H., Curtis Jenkins, G. and Basharan, H. (1995) 'The training needs of counsellors in primary medical care', *Journal of Mental Health*, 4: 205–9.

Epston, D. and White, M. (1990) *Narrative Means to Therapeutic Ends*, New York: Norton.

Fitzgerald, P. and Murphy, A. (1997) 'Counsellor training placements', *Medical Monitor*, May: 55–6.

Gilbert, M. and Shmukler, D. (1996) *Brief Therapy with Couples*, Chichester: Wiley.

Henderson, Penny (1995) 'Management of choice: using a male and female counsellor team in general practice', unpublished paper.

Hoag, L. (1992) 'Psychotherapy in the general practice surgery', *British Journal of Psychotherapy*, 8 (4): 417–29.

Inskipp, F. and Proctor, B. (1995) *Making the Most of Supervision*, Part 2, Twickenham: Cascade Publications.

Jones, H., Murphy, A., Neaman, G., Tollecache, R. and Vasserman, D. (1994) 'Psychotherapy and counselling in a GP practice: making use of the setting', *Journal of General Practice*, 10 (4): 543–51.

Kendrick, T., Sibbald, B., Addington Hall, J., Renneman, D. and Freeling, P. (1993) 'Distribution of mental health professionals working on site in English and Welsh General Practices', *British Medical Journal*, 307: 544–6.

Lees, J. (1997) 'An approach to counselling in GP surgeries', *Psychodynamic Counselling*, 3 (1): 33–48.

Lethem, J. (1994) *Moved to Tears, Moved to Action: Solution Focused Brief Therapy with Women and Children*, London: Brief Therapy Press.

Mathers, N., Jones, N. and Hannay, D. (1995) 'Heartsink patients: a study of their General Practitioners', *British Journal of General Practice*, 45: 293–6.

Mearns, D. (1994) *Developing Person-Centred Counselling*, London: Sage.

Nias, J. (1996) 'Responsibility and partnership in the primary school', in P. Taylor and S. Mullen (eds) *The Primary Professional*, Birmingham: Educational Partners.

O'Connell, B. and Jones, C. (1997) 'Solution focused supervision', *Counselling*, 8 (4) (November): 289–92.

Orbach, S. (1997) 'Shrink rap', *Guardian*, 7 June.

Schon, D. (1987) *Educating the Reflective Practitioner*, San Francisco, CA: Jossey Bass.
Speirs, R. and Jewell, T. (1995) 'One counsellor 2 practices', *British Journal of General Practice*, 45: 31–3.
Stern, D. (1997) John Bowlby Memorial Lecture, March, London.
Woodhouse, D. and Pengelly, P. (1991) *Anxiety and the Dynamics of Collaboration*, Aberdeen: Aberdeen University Press.

6 Supervision in educational settings

Margaret Tholstrup

Supervising counsellors and psychotherapists in an educational setting presents a series of unique challenges to the supervision practitioner. Among those discussed in this chapter are:

- the preponderantly young population which presents itself for counselling;
- the seasonal fluctuation in client load;
- the academic and maturational demands imposed on students by the educational setting;
- how organizational policy and politics are mirrored by lines of responsibility between the counselling provision and the setting, and by issues of accountability, accessibility, confidentiality and evaluation.

Finally, a case study illustrates the unique supervision issues endemic in this setting.

The primary aim of an educational setting is to impart knowledge, and sometimes training, to students. Settings vary from those where education is compulsory and full-time (primary and secondary schools), voluntary and usually full-time such as colleges and universities, and part-time adult education or short-term vocational trainings. Many offer some form of counselling to students, be it career counselling, pastoral counselling or personal development/crisis counselling. In addition, some offer counselling or learning support which focuses primarily on how to study effectively or complete academic assignments. In this chapter, counselling is defined as the help sought to deal with intra-psychic or interpersonal issues.

Counselling provision within educational settings varies and is not dependent upon the educational context. It includes counselling as:

- an integral part of the setting, funded by the institution for its students and staff as part of its welfare services;
- a more informal arrangement whereby a counsellor is available and on the premises regularly (frequently under the auspices of the medical service); or
- contracted out to a private practitioner or counselling service in the area.

In this chapter I will focus primarily on the institution providing higher education to full-time students because it is the setting of the majority of counselling services in education, though issues particular to other educational settings will also be considered.

Characteristics of the setting and clientele

One of the unique characteristics of educational settings is the transient nature of its customers: students come for a limited time to learn something specific or gain a qualification before moving on. This ebb and flow of people results in only a partial commitment to the organization, though this is less typical of full-time students. The educational setting provides a hiatus during which the full-time, usually young, student has the opportunity to develop a knowledge base in order to increase employment opportunities later in life. (The particular issues facing counsellors in compulsory education are considered separately in the section on 'The under-age student', page 118.)

Another characteristic of the educational setting is the average age of the population. Students are usually young, although the number of non-traditional students seeking further education is growing. The average age varies with the setting; for the most part younger students are engaged in full-time education, while older ones seek a part-time qualification or a full-time one scheduled around work and home commitments.

A third characteristic of the setting is that much of its population will be living away from home, perhaps for the first time, and experiencing the lack of external restraints that this implies, as well as exploring issues of identity, intimacy and sexuality (Erikson 1963). Full-time students live in halls or lodgings, and negotiate moral and ethical decisions and dilemmas without the ready recourse to parents or other significant, known, authority figures.

Staff are a more stable component of an educational setting as their involvement is differently motivated, that is, by employment over the long term. As a result they have more loyalty and therefore contribute more consistently to the organization. Staff, like students, also experience considerable variation in the pressure of work, with peaks around exams and course preparation time and troughs during long summer holidays. This pattern is changing as the pressure to do research and maximize the use of existing facilities increases in today's hothouse academic environment.

Type of counsellor

The Student Counselling Service which I helped set up in a higher education setting had two different types of counsellors: qualified counsellors employed by the college and counsellors-in-training whose work was supervised by the staff counsellors. The latter, when applying to work as trainees in the counselling service, submitted a current c.v. and two references, and underwent on interview with the qualified counsellors. They undertook a year's placement with the Service, which provided regular client contact (between one and eight hours per week), free supervision and three training meetings during the course of the year. Counsellors on placement were trained in the Service's administrative systems (writing and submitting case notes, booking rooms etc.) before seeing any clients. The placement contract was re-negotiable once for an additional year, though the supervisor changed.

In order to get the best for themselves and provide the best for their student clients, trainee counsellors working in educational setting should:

- have considerable previous experience, either personal or professional, of young people;
- understand the unique complexities and demands of an educational setting, such as peak pressure time around exams and essay deadlines;
- have free time during the day when students prefer to be seen (travelling between sites at night presents issues of personal safety);
- have flexible schedules as student timetables usually change during the year.

The advantages of a placement in an educational setting include:

- free supervision (frequently in a group with trainees from the same course);
- flexibility for those able to work during the day;
- a guaranteed source of interesting, usually young, clients who present with a variety of issues, and 'get better' quickly or at least show quantifiable change quite rapidly.

Other advantages can include:

- no prescribed time limit to counselling contracts;
- no previous experience of counselling, if there is in-house supervision.

Types of supervision

Types of supervision offered to counsellors in an educational setting vary. Some include:

1. Supervision of sessional counsellors who provide counselling for students and/or staff of the institution. This type of supervision is independently contracted for, is external to (though may be funded by) the institution, and does not include managerial responsibility.
2. Supervision of an in-house counselling service managed by permanent staff. For ethical reasons the Association for Student Counselling requires that supervisors of this type of counsellor come from outside the institution (Association for Student Counselling (undated a): 9). Supervision could be of casework, supervision of supervision or team supervision, but there is no casework responsibility.
3. Supervision of counsellors on a time-limited placement within an in-house service. Placement counsellors may be attending professional training courses or already be qualified and keen to keep current their counselling skills. Supervision is provided in exchange for voluntary counselling hours, is carried out by the permanent staff, and covers both casework and managerial issues.
4. Supervision of trainee counsellors as an integral part of their course. The supervisor is a member of the course staff and has little or no connection with the trainee's placement. This type of supervision is developmental (of the trainee) and focuses

on issues such as setting up a professional relationship, professional boundaries, codes of ethics and practice. The supervisor has no managerial responsibility for client work.

5.   Supervision arranged by a training course which pays the supervisor to supervise students who are charged separately for supervision. The course has no responsibility for the supervision, though the supervisor must be known as an ethical practitioner and is responsible for their own supervision of supervision. There is an inherent potential for dual relationships which needs monitoring, especially if the supervisor is also a member of the teaching staff.

Because the majority of issues which arise in supervision in an educational setting occur in options 2 and 3 above, they will form the focus of this chapter. To minimize confusion, 'student' will denote a student of the institution and be used interchangeably with 'client'. 'Supervisee' will be the counsellor on placement with the in-house service, while 'supervisor' is also the staff counsellor.

Role/task of supervisor

There are four important issues to consider in the supervising of an ethical counselling service in an educational setting: accountability, accessibility, confidentiality and evaluation. Staff counsellors, in their roles as supervisors, hold the tension between the demands of students for counselling, the provision of an ethical and accountable service, the efficient and effective running of this service and the learning needs of counsellors on placement. It is important that the supervisor holds both managerial responsibility for the ethical functioning of placement counsellors and casework responsibility for client work. This juggling act necessitates frequent monitoring, and becomes a major subject for discussion at staff meetings, team supervision and supervision of supervision.

Accountability

As supervisors, staff counsellors exercise managerial responsibility for the quality of counselling work provided by counsellors on placement by:

1. Making all decisions jointly, including who is accepted on placement and how to make referrals to them. They share both supervision of client work and supervision of supervision with an outside supervisor. Their aim is to provide safe provision for the students who come for help, and assurance to their employers, to whom they are responsible, of the ethical standard of counselling provided by the Service.

2. Monitoring the quality of the work carried out by placement counsellors. This is done in regular, weekly supervision sessions, and by the collecting and reading of weekly case notes written by the placement counsellors on each client. Monitoring how effectively administrative procedures are followed continues both in weekly supervision groups and in the regular reading of case notes. Three annual team meetings and regular contact with the receptionist/secretary of the Service provide placement trainees with a feeling of belonging to, and thus accountability to, the Student Counselling Service.

3. Assessing the development of the placement counsellor. The supervisor is responsible to the counselling trainee for sufficient client hours to meet the demands of their training course, and helps the placement counsellor mature as a competent counsellor.

The issue of accountability becomes more complex when the placement counsellor has completed training and wants to maintain counselling skills by seeing clients part-time. While the supervisor maintains managerial responsibility for client work, he/she allows the counsellor casework responsibility for client work, commensurate to the placement counsellor's level of training. The supervisor needs to contract carefully with the placement counsellor, so that issues of countertransference or parallel process which arise in supervision are identified and dealt with appropriately. In one instance, a volunteer counsellor found that her client was triggering off too many of her own issues to continue working effectively. Her supervisor asked her to choose between resuming personal therapy or discontinuing her placement; she chose the latter.

Accessibility

Accessibility extends in two directions: first, the staff supervisor needs to ensure the Service is experienced as accessible to students. Prompt follow-up of referrals to placement counsellors helps achieve this. When trainee counsellors and students referred to them cannot find a mutually convenient time to meet, the supervisor asks to be informed immediately to minimize the time necessary to make alternative arrangements.

In addition, staff counsellors are accessible to the placement counsellors for supervision outside of regular supervision time. Trainees have their supervisor's home phone number and, in an emergency, whichever supervisor is currently available provides help or advice. Not only is this an aspect of accessibility, but one which also ensures accountability.

Confidentiality

In an educational setting, where the primary aim of both students and staff is that students stay on their courses, confidentiality becomes a major issue. Anxious to keep up student numbers on his course, a tutor who has referred a distraught student who is considering leaving could phone and ask how the student is doing in counselling. At all meetings and supervision sessions, the importance of keeping addresses and names separate from case notes is stressed as is the safe delivery of case notes to the Service.

At the initial assessment, all students are asked for the name and address of their GP who will only be contacted in an emergency and with the knowledge, though not necessarily the permission, of the student. Around exam times, some students want letters from their counsellors asking for special consideration in exams or overdue assignments. Placement counsellors draft their own letters, which are typed by the secretary on headed paper and signed by the counsellor before being handed to the student. These letters are usually vague in nature, and their purpose is to corroborate that the student is experiencing difficulties for which they are seeking help.

Evaluation

Staff supervisors are responsible for evaluating the quality of the service delivered to students via trainees' contributions to, and openness to learning in, supervision. And, vice versa, the supervisor's effectiveness both as a supervisor and as an effective manager of an efficient and responsive Service needs evaluating. Placement counsellors annually give feedback to the Service, either verbally or in writing, about the quality of supervision they have received. This helps to make the Service a more responsible and responsive placement for all counsellors. The inherent risk for trainees is whether they can be totally honest, as what they say may reflect on any request for future references; anonymous answers are preferable.

Trainees need regular supervision reports for their courses which involves supervisors in writing an assessment of each of them. One way of accomplishing this effectively is by asking supervisees to evaluate themselves (and, on occasion, fellow supervisees in a group), then discussing similarities and differences. Supervisees read and agree with their reports before signing them, so any differences of opinion can be negotiated and relevant changes incorporated in the final document.

Unique supervision issues

The unique issues which arise when supervising in an educational context will be discussed in terms of the organization, the supervisor and the counsellor.

The organization

The aim of any educational setting is to provide education to students as efficiently as possible with the minimum of aggravation. The risk for counselling is to be perceived as a resource for 'sorting out' problem students. A counselling service needs to clarify whether it is willing to act in this paternalistic and quasi-disciplinary role. For example, if two young men caught setting off a fire extinguisher very early one morning are required, as a condition for remaining in college, to attend a session of counselling, is this an appropriate use of counselling provision? Can tutors insist on knowing what transpires in counselling sessions, or even whether the student has kept the appointment for counselling? Both client and counsellor can be cajoled into divulging what is happening in counselling with the most well-meaning purposes in mind. This is most likely to occur when there is a strong transferential urge to protect or cosset the new student. The situation is different when the student is younger than 18 (see 'The under-age student', page 118).

Another organizational issue is the impact on the counselling service of organizational politics and policy. A measure of this is how independent the counselling provision is in providing a service focused primarily on student needs. The organization wants to keep students in college in order to obtain government funding, yet students use counselling to help resolve uncertainties about whether to pursue further education. The supervisor needs to support the counsellor to facilitate the student in making an independent decision and supporting self-determination. Any implicit or explicit demand to keep students enrolled in the institution needs examining.

Supervision provides a forum for devising strategies to counter-act the poor communication frequently endemic in educational settings. Some institutions may be spread across several sites or once have been separate colleges; this can lead to strained or non-existent communication between departments or colleges. The impact of decisions made at one location might not take into account the effect on those at other campuses. One placement counsellor walked into her regular counselling room during the holidays to find workmen tearing out the carpet and painting the walls – her client was expected in ten minutes. No one had told the Service (on another site) of the appropriation of the room and its intended new use as an office! Space and accommodation are frequently sources of strife within an educational setting, as in the above example. Another scenario had a student waiting for her counselling appointment in an empty room when two women with clipboards and tape measures walked in discussing the best use of the room for the following term. The trainee counsellor was taken aback when his client recounted the story, and the issue erupted in supervision later that day. In both situations the super-visor investigated the matter, pursued it through the organiza-tional hierarchy and was able to calm everyone's fears when she reported back to the group. Here the supervisor was modelling clear communication with the organization and her supervisees.

The educational organization may also expect the in-house counselling provision to meet the needs of all students coming for counselling: tutors phone with distressed students crying in their rooms, asking that they be seen immediately, or a student suffers a sudden bereavement or fails an exam, and must see a counsellor at once! The supervisor as staff counsellor has to balance the most efficient use of the service with fairness to all who contact it for help. Keeping slots clear for these emergencies while other students are phoning or coming in with pressing issues is a very difficult process: how does the counsellor decide which is the emergency, when every call sounds like one? A list of alternative services for emergencies, such as the chaplains, personal tutors, hall reps, student union welfare officers or the local GP is helpful. External agencies available out of hours such as hospital casualty, the Samaritans, rape crisis lines and the medical service are useful for resident students.

The organization may expect the in-house Counselling Service to provide counselling for staff, which raises an issue of confidentiality: the counselling team are also members of staff and meet other staff in informal settings such as the cafeteria or library, or on committees or official business. One option is to see staff as a one-off in an emergency, then refer them outside the institution for further counselling. Confidentiality is assured if staff are not offered counselling within the organization.

The supervisor

Two of the most important issues for the supervisor in an educational setting are who pays for the supervision and to whom the supervisor is responsible. Those whose supervision is external and independently contracted can choose their own supervisor and contract that they submit an invoice directly to the institution. All that is required of the supervisor is that he/she is appropriately qualified and the staff team happy with their choice. Rarely, if ever, does the organization meet the supervisor and vice versa. This maintains the confidentiality of the staff supervisor, who then feels free to bring organizational issues to supervision (Carroll 1996).

Counsellors supervising placement counsellors as part of their contracted employment provide a cheap and efficient way for the educational setting to obtain additional counselling provision on a shoestring. Some of the risks to the supervisory process of this policy are:

1. Not all clients are brought regularly to supervision although the supervisor remains accountable to the organization for all counselling work. One option for overcoming this problem is for the supervisor to read all case notes written by the trainee

counsellors regularly, so he/she maintains some ongoing awareness of what is occurring in the counselling relationship.

2. The placement counsellor puts pressure on the supervisor for more clients in order to meet course requirements of a specified number of client hours per year. The educational setting makes this situation unique because of the aforementioned ebb and flow of counselling demand and scheduling changes within the year. In addition, the supervisor may be reluctant to pass further clients to the supervisee because those clients available are not suitable for the counsellor (usually because of the trainee's lack of experience) or their schedules do not match. This situation is talked through in supervision, and either patience advised, or, in the second case, the trainee negotiates additional counselling time.

3. The trainee, feeling the pressures of combining a training course with a personal life and a job, decides not to take on any new clients. The supervisor clarifies the reasons for this decision, but is faced with the need to find suitable provision either with another placement or staff counsellor. This becomes a problem around the peak pressure times of exams and assignment deadlines.

Another issue for the supervisor is how to manage limited group supervision time; there needs to be adequate provision for clinical or casework supervision while not neglecting administrative or managerial issues. Unless there is a crisis with a client, I prefer to deal with concrete managerial issues first, on the assumption that they can be dealt with more rapidly, and leave the major part of the supervision session for casework discussion. This assumption does not always reflect actuality; placement counsellors can feel either that they are not getting enough individual supervision time or that their caseloads require more time than they are allocated. In this scenario the supervisor holds a tension between the demands of an ethical and efficient service and still meeting the developmental and safety needs of supervisees.

The relationship between what Bernard and Goodyear call the 'site supervisor' (the Service supervisor in this context) and the 'university supervisor' (the course tutor) is an interesting one needing careful and clear negotiation for the maximum benefit of the trainee counsellor (1992: 159–64). Until now the focus has been on the tension between the service provider (the counsellors on placement) and the customers/consumers of the service (the students), which is held and managed by the supervisor. Another dimension is added when the placement counsellor is also on a counselling course; this relationship requires negotiation and careful contracting so both parties are clear about their respective responsibilities to the trainee counsellor and to each other to minimize misunderstandings. If the trainee requires supervision in the particular orientation of the course which the placement cannot provide, the supervisor retains managerial responsibility and accountability for all client work carried out under the auspices of the Counselling Service.

The supervisor decides the format for supervision of placement counsellors, whether it is individual or group. The advantage of group supervision is partly financial, in that the supervisor maximizes the use of time by seeing more placement counsellors, but also encourages a sense of connection with the Service and accountability to it. As well as helping placement counsellors to become more competent and to work collaboratively, supervision provides a powerful learning environment where both managerial and personal development issues are aired while counsellors are supported and challenged. Even completing counsellor evaluations required by training courses is more useful in a group, as everyone learns how to give and receive feedback in a supportive and facilitating way.

The counsellor

Counsellors working in an educational setting face several issues specific to the setting which can challenge their belief system, such as young people's desire to experiment with drugs, alcohol and sex. Though these practices can be dangerous, young people may believe they are immortal and that the potentially harmful consequences of such behaviour will not affect them. The supervisor helps the counsellor by discussing any risks implicit in the specific behaviour so that the counsellor can try to hold the balance between keeping what could be a fragile client in counselling and imposing a ban on any dangerous behaviour. The counsellor is encouraged to bear in mind that students are adults, and once informed of the risks of the course they are pursuing, have the right to choose whether to continue doing so. A degree of latitude is tolerable: one counsellor contracted with her client, a regular cannabis smoker, not to have a 'joint' on the day of her counselling session.

Student issues can trigger feelings of anger and helplessness in the counsellor: students with very little money, working three days a week stacking shelves to supplement the remnants of a student loan can jeopardize their education because they are too tired to meet academic deadlines. Financial and academic survival take precedence over self-exploration, so, though the counsellor knows the safe container of counselling can help the student cope, students have more pressing priorities which need acknowledging. Supervision is a forum to vent the counsellor's feelings of frustration and rage.

Another example is the often-repeated story of parents separating or selling the family home as the young person leaves for college. Although this may be healthier for the individuals involved and the student may ultimately be relieved, Mother now shares a two-bedroom flat with boyfriend and two siblings, and communication with Father broke down long ago, so where does she go when college accommodation closes over the holidays? Where is home? The counsellor empathizing with the student finds him- or herself caught in powerful countertransferential reactions which surface in supervision. The supervisor is clear about their own feelings about divorce, parental responsibilities and the limits of the caring relationship to facilitate the counsellor's exploration of their own.

For many students this will be their first experience of counselling, and, even when carefully instructed in the conventions (arriving on time, the length of the counselling hour, cancelling early), they may disappear after a few, or even one, session(s). Counsellors can underestimate the impact of just a few sessions, believing that the counselling contract needs to be completed to have worked. The student may, however, gain immeasurably from this short contact and have sufficient insight to enable him or her to face future difficulties more effectively. In this scenario supervisors help counsellors trust the process and allow the student to go.

Placement counsellors who are also trainees on a counselling course can identify strongly with the students whom they are seeing for counselling, especially if they are both struggling with similar issues such as the difficulty of writing essays or completing assignments on time. This potential exists in any counselling setting, but it is especially poignant when both are studying in the same institution. An inadvertent meeting in the library triggers issues for both, but usually more for the beginning counsellor, and these are fruitfully aired in supervision. The supervisor in the educational setting needs to be alert to the potential for this type of countertransference.

Specialized client groups

Those with severe psychological or psychiatric distress

Over the past few years there has been a noticeable increase in the number of students with severe psychological or psychiatric issues in education. The reason for this is unclear, but the growth is sufficiently great to elicit a pamphlet from the Association for Student Counselling entitled *Working with Disturbed and Disturbing Students* (undated b). It highlights the complexities presented to counsellors when these students come for counselling.

The first important thing for the counsellor to ascertain is who made the referral, whether it was the student or a third party, and whether a counselling referral, as opposed to a medical or psychiatric one, was the correct one to make. On the other hand, the institution could be expecting the counsellor to sort out or contain the 'problem' student in the absence of another alternative. This type of student needs careful assessing to ascertain the best category of help for them.

If the student is accepted for counselling, the staff counsellors need to decide who will take him or her on. The institution assumes that the most experienced counsellors will see the more disturbed clients; the risk is that their caseload becomes full of these demanding, difficult clients, with burnout a distinct possibility.

The supervisor has several roles in this situation: one is to assess the counsellor's overall caseload, and ascertain that the counsellor is not overloaded by the quantity and type of client they are seeing. If the counsellor is inexperienced, the supervisor needs to be especially aware of whether the counsellor is accurately assessing the client's level of distress or disturbance – the counsellor may have difficulty realizing how damaged or dangerous a client is, and believe they can cope with anything or anyone. Another role is to work with the counsellor to make policy decisions about how to handle such referrals in a way which is both safe and helpful to client and counsellor. This may mean limiting the number of disturbed or disturbing clients seen by the counselling provision, and finding other sources to which they can be referred. Building up relationships with outside agencies, such as medical services and psychiatric in-patient units, is especially useful. Another option is to provide, with the counsellor, training for other staff in how to handle difficult students.

Perhaps the supervisor's most important task is to focus on institutional dynamics and ascertain whether the counselling provision is being used as a dumping ground for students who are too difficult or disturbed to be contained by other entities within the institution. A possibility is that others in the educational setting are too scared of these students or do not know how to handle them. The assumption is that counsellors have this expertise, with the result that everyone considered a 'problem' is sent in their direction.

The under-age student

Supervising counsellors working in school settings present a separate set of supervision issues, though many of those discussed above are also pertinent (Henderson 1994). Unique tasks include deciding how much of what is revealed in counselling is confidential communication, and how much should be discussed with other authorities. What happens when the under-16 student divulges something which, by law, must be reported to Social Services, such as sexual abuse? The supervisor's role in this situation is to support the counsellor in deciding how best to protect the best interests of the child, including approaching the relevant statutory body. The supervisor's first priority is to prevent harm, and this is an important example of when to focus on this supervisory responsibility. Approaching the authorities immediately is not necessarily the best option in the short term, but ensuring the safety of the child is always paramount.

The counsellor also takes on the role of advocate for the young person, while respecting their opinions and supporting them in making independent decisions about their lives. One example is in the case of bullying, where the counsellor helps empower the student, where feasible, to take action on their own. Where it is not, confidentiality can be broken in the better interests of the child. Being used as a sounding board to test out opinions and actions is especially appropriate for counsellors of clients of this age group, and supervisors can help counsellors to accept this. All counselling does not need to be deep and insightful, and in this situation the developmental aspect is more important.

Case study

A supervision group of three placement counsellors and supervisor meets for one-and-a-half hours in a room of the in-house, fully funded Counselling Service. Mary has been supervising groups of placement counsellors for three years. Gerald, a member of staff in another educational setting, is on a three-year humanistic counselling training; he has just started seeing clients, and has two. Sue completed her training last year and wants to maintain her counselling skills, so sees two clients weekly. Pat, enrolled on a psychotherapy training course, needs to see at least five clients per week; she currently sees four.

The end of the first term approaches, and Gerald and Pat meet with Mary individually as supervision reports are due immediately after the holidays. Gerald divulges that he is considering leaving his marriage because he is having an affair with a student: he told the group when Mary was absent the previous week, and asked them to keep it a secret. Mary is concerned about boundary issues, but Gerald assures her the student is not a client. Mary senses a power play on Gerald's part in divulging this information to the group and getting them to agree to keep it secret: is her authority as supervisor being undermined? She and Gerald contract to discuss the issue openly at their next supervision. Mary is also worried about the way in which he speaks of the student, and asks him whether he has taken this relationship to his personal therapy; he hasn't, but agrees he will. He is absent at the next meeting, the final one before the holidays.

In this group, Sue presents her work with one of her clients, a first-year student whose father left three years ago and whose mother's boyfriend refuses to have her in the house – she has nowhere to go over the holidays and cannot afford temporary accommodation. Sue tells the group she wanted to offer the student a room in her own home, then starts to cry as she talks of her own abuse, as an adolescent, by a new stepfather: she has never spoken of this before. When Mary suggests she re-enter personal therapy to get support and disentangle her issues from her client's, Sue says another staff counsellor, a close friend, promised she would not have to go into therapy while on placement: not only can she not afford it, but she found her previous experience abusive.

Pat then talks about a client she has seen several times, a second-year student who has just divulged that she is working as a 'hostess' in a private club to help finance her course, but is now enjoying having some money to spend. Mary elicits Pat's angry countertransferential feelings that a student needs to earn money in this way in order to complete her education, even though this is not an issue for the student. Pat is also concerned for her client's safety; one of her 'regulars' has become quite demanding by asking her not to see anyone else and move in with him. She does not want to do this as she wants to finish college and become a fashion designer, but she saw him in the library the other day, and is afraid he may be stalking her. Mary and Pat come up with strategies to help Pat empower her client to protect herself while Sue becomes angry because, as a member of the administrative staff, she knows how much students spend in the bar each night.

Later in the day, as Mary writes the supervision reports, she suddenly wonders whether Gerald might be the man Pat's client is referring to.

The above case study highlights some issues which are typical of supervision in an educational setting. These are:

- the potential for boundary violations when counselling trainees see students from the same setting as clients;
- poor communication between staff and prospective placement counsellors;
- personal issues which are stirred up when working with young people;
- the seasonal shift in workload between holidays and term time, whether this is in the demand for counselling and supervision, or more directly, of academic deadlines;
- client issues related to divorce or separation of parents, and how these come into focus at holiday times;

- organizational issues that impact on students and their lives, for example college fees, having to supplement maintenance grants;
- a sense of intertwined relationships and responsibilities.

Recommendations for training supervisors

Very little has been written about supervising in educational settings. Bernard and Goodyear (1992) devote part of a chapter on 'Administrative Tasks' to the topics of 'training systems', 'the university supervisor' and 'the field site supervisor'. These three sections deal with some of the issues experienced in supervising in educational settings and highlight the importance of clear contracting and communication between training course and placement. In this reference the university supervisor is actually the course supervisor or placement co-ordinator, while the role of the site supervisor relates more closely to the supervisor in an educational setting, as described in this chapter.

My recommendations for preparing supervisors to work in an educational setting include:

- experience of counselling in an educational setting in order to understand its unique dynamics and demands;
- an understanding of the potential for parallel processing between the organization, supervision, the counselling provision and its clientele;
- an ability to work flexibly, as the demand for counselling and supervision waxes and wanes during the academic year;
- an appreciation of the role of the counselling provision within the educational setting: how it is seen, what the expectations are of the counsellors and of the organization, and what bearing they have on reality;
- tact and diplomacy to deal with other entities within and outside the educational setting, and an understanding of their relationship to the counselling provision;
- some experience of what is expected of supervisors of case-work in relation to training courses, when placement counsellors are seeing clients as part of counselling training;
- the ability to contract clearly and accurately, both verbally and, when necessary, in writing;

- an understanding of administrative systems to deal with the demands of managerial supervision and the need to maintain effective and responsive systems;
- the ability to work effectively as a member of a team of counsellors.

Several of these tasks are common to all types of supervision, but some are of particular importance to the supervisor in an educational setting.

Conclusion

Supervisors working in educational settings face a series of unique challenges which call for high levels of skill and professionalism. Paramount among these is the fluctuation in demand for counselling and supervision; at peak times there are not enough hours in the day, while holidays are necessary for recuperation and setting in place strategies for delivering a more effective service next time. The clientele, while demanding, are interesting to work with and the changes they frequently exhibit make the work satisfying. Continual change in both clients and placement counsellors challenge the supervisor's accepted ways of practising and keep them on their toes. Supervising in an educational setting is exhausting, stimulating, challenging and, most importantly, rewarding.

References

Association for Student Counselling (undated a) *Advisory Service to Institutions*. Rugby: BAC.

Association for Student Counselling (undated b) *Working with Disturbed and Disturbing Students*, Advisory Service Discussion paper. Rugby: BAC.

Bernard, J.M. and Goodyear, R.K. (1992) *Fundamentals of Clinical Supervision*. Boston, MA: Allyn & Bacon.

Carroll, M. (1996) *Workplace Counselling*. London: Sage.

Erikson, E. (1963) *Childhood and Society*. New York: Norton.

Henderson, P. (1994) *Supervision of School Counselors*. Greensboro, NC: Eric Digest.

7 Supervision of school counsellors in Israel: setting up a network of supervision

Shoshana Hellman

History of school counselling in Israel

In 1962 the Ministry of Education in Israel decided to introduce counsellors to the school system. In 1964, 43 counsellor–teachers started their work in elementary schools and in special education classes mostly in needy areas. Today there are more than 2,500 school counsellors in the country, at least half of them with an MA degree in counselling. Most of them have a teaching certificate and also function as teachers.

From the beginning school counsellors at all levels of experience were provided with supervision by the Ministry of Education. Supervision was less structured and was given according to needs. Later, when the number of counsellors grew, the number of supervisors also increased accordingly and supervision was given in a more structured and systematic manner. Today there are twenty-five supervisors appointed by the Ministry of Education. All of the supervisors have at least an MA degree in counselling, experience as counsellors and teachers, and academic training in supervision. Supervision for school counsellors includes individual supervision, group supervision and ongoing in-service workshops and training. The supervisors are part of the Department of Counselling and Psychological Services in the Ministry of Education ('Sheffy').

The department is responsible for all counsellors and psychologists working in the school system, and its general functions include:

- statement and implementation of the counselling and psychological policy in Israeli schools (including Arab–Israeli schools);
- integration of this policy with the general policy of education in Israel through committees and projects in the schools;
- development of a comprehensive counselling and guidance programme;
- administrative and professional responsibility for the development of the supervisors.

Figure 7.1 shows the structure of the Psychological and Counselling Services in Israel – 'Sheffy' – which includes three branches

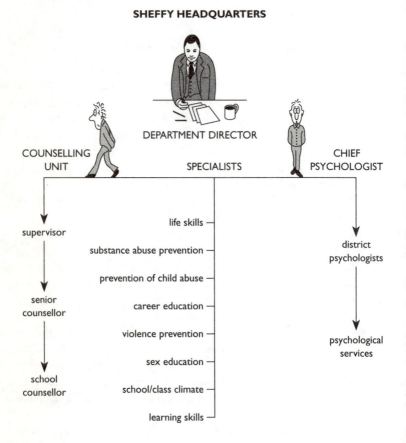

Figure 7.1   *Overview of the department of counselling and psychological services*

(sections): counselling, psychology and counselling programmes. Each branch is headed by a person responsible for the professional development of the supervisors in that section.

Model of supervision of school counsellors in Israel

Types and goals of supervision

According to the Association for Counsellor Education and Supervision (ACES 1995) the responsibilities of counselling supervisors include responsibilities in clinical supervision and in administrative supervision.

Administrative supervision refers to those supervisory activities that increase the efficiency of the delivery of counselling services. It could be time-management and the counsellors' relationship with the staff. Clinical supervision includes the supportive and educative activities of the supervisor designed to improve the application of counselling theory and technique directly to clients. When applied to school counselling, it is defined by Roberts and Borders (1994) as supervision which focuses on enhancing counsellors' clinical knowledge and skill working with students in individual or group counselling sessions, and in consultation with parents and teachers.

The third type of supervision is developmental supervision (Barret and Schmidt 1986; Schmidt 1990), referring to supervision focused on programme development, implementation and co-ordination such as classroom guidance.

'Sheffy' is responsible for these three modes of supervision in relation to its supervisors, and the supervisors are also involved in all these types of supervision.

The following general goals of supervision as defined by Boyd (1987) and Roberts and Borders (1994) are also relevant for Israel:

1. Facilitation and enhancement of the counsellor's personal and professional development.
2. Promotion of the competency of the counsellor and development of specific counselling skills.
3. Promotion of accountable counselling and guidance services and programmes.
4. Professional support and avoidance of burnout.

In the United States, supervision for practising counsellors, particularly school counsellors, is non-existent (Borders and Schmidt 1992; Schmidt 1990), even though most counsellors surveyed indicated a desire for supervision, in particular from a counsellor who had had additional training in supervision (Borders and Usher 1992). In Britain, on the other hand, there is life-long supervision for counsellors as included in the British Association for Counselling Code of Ethics.

In Israel, because counselling supervisors were appointed by the Ministry of Education to cover all schools, supervision is mandatory for all school counsellors.

Structure of supervision

The supervisor is appointed to a district where he is responsible for the supervision of the counsellors in all school settings (elementary, middle and high school, including special education). Since at times a supervisor is responsible for a considerable number of counsellors in a large area of the country, he is helped by senior counsellors who function as supervisors and who are trained to do so at university.

Recently programme development also became an important part of the counsellor's work. Counsellors are involved in prevention programmes such as violence prevention, drug and alcohol abuse prevention, and developmental programmes such as career development, sex education, learning skills and life skills. Each of these areas is headed by an 'expert supervisor' in the field and for each area there are 'specialist counsellors' (usually senior counsellors) trained in specific programmes, who provide supervision and consultation to the counsellors and schools.

In summary

The counselling supervisor – appointed by the Ministry of Education. Reports professionally to the Department of Counselling and Psychological Services in the Ministry. Responsible for the supervision of school counsellors in large areas of the country. Is also responsible for the formation of policy for counselling in Israel.

The senior counsellor-supervisor – appointed by the counselling supervisor. Responsible for individual supervision of a few counsellors and also at times group supervision of small groups of counsellors. Usually functions as a counsellor in addition. Completed a specialized training in supervision.

The expert supervisor – heads a programme area such as life skills, violence prevention or other speciality areas. Responsible for implementing the programmes in the schools. Appointed by the Ministry of Education.

The specialist counsellor/supervisor – appointed by head of particular specialization ('expert' supervisor). Provides supervision or consultation individually or in groups regarding prevention programmes or developmental counselling programmes. Specialized in one of the programmes in a training course. Usually functions as a counsellor in addition to the specialization.

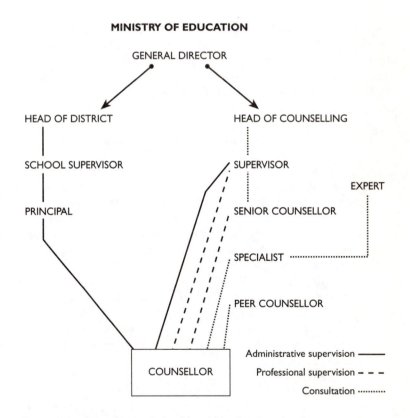

Figure 7.2 *Supervisory relationship within the educational system*

The counsellor – functions also as a teacher at times and is supervised administratively by the principal of the school and also by the supervisor of the school, who is in charge of the professional development of all the teachers and of the principal.

Roles of the counsellor and modes of supervision

In order to facilitate the professional development of the counsellor in a more systematic manner and provide him or her with appropriate supervisory interventions, the Ministry of Education requested the Department of Counselling and Psychological Services to define the role of the counsellor in Israel and design a structured model of supervision.

The major roles of the counsellor as identified in the literature (Bernstein et al. 1994; Campbell 1992) and which were also applied to the Israeli counsellor are: (a) individual counselling, (b) classroom guidance, (c) group counselling, (d) consultation with teachers, parents, administrators, (e) organizational consultation, (f) co-ordination and work in a team, (g) transitions (to a different school – high school, etc.), (h) crisis intervention (especially typical of the work of an Israeli counsellor).

Because of this variety of roles there are also various modes of supervision:

1. Individual supervision in which the counsellor presents the case to the supervisor, using video or audiotape and the supervisor consults with the counsellor in managing the individual session or is engaged in an ongoing supervision of the case.
2. In cases of classroom guidance the presence of the supervisor in the class and the review after the class is another way of supervision. This supervision can also be given by a supervisor specializing in programme development and counselling programmes.
3. Group supervision, moderated by the supervisor or the senior counsellor, in which members of the group present cases and consult each other.
4. Peer-group supervision was developed recently. It is a less threatening approach to self-examination and professional growth. Peer groups can provide support as well as enhance skills and promote professional development (Benshoff and Paisley 1996; Crutchfield and Borders 1997).

Difficulties in supervision

As a result of the uniqueness of the school counselling work in Israel and the structure of the supervision network, several difficulties are beginning to emerge.

In a country where terrorist attacks happen on a frequent basis, children at a very young age are exposed to buses exploding and constant crisis situations. Israel also has a very high rate of fatal car accidents because of the stressfulness of life and counsellors often feel helpless and unprepared for these events. Specific counselling interventions are needed both for the very young and for parents and the community.

Because of the country's political situation, crisis intervention is a critical component of the counsellor's work and in-service training workshops are provided on a continuous basis. Special guidelines as to what to do in such cases are given to each counsellor and books with special activities for such events are provided. There is nevertheless always a sense of lack of preparation for these events and this area becomes a major concern of counsellors and supervisors.

Second, cases of domestic violence are also escalating, and violence in general is a big problem. Here the counsellor is part of a team, and has to work closely with the social services, police, community or municipal services and others. The skill of co-ordinating a team and of working as a member of one is very important for counselling and supervision.

Third, the socio-political climate also has an effect on counselling and supervision. The conflict between various factions in Israeli society is affecting schools. The disparity between left and right (settlers), and between religious and non-religious people, culminating in the political assassination of the Israeli Prime Minister, had an immense effect on youngsters in Israel. The phenomenon of 'candle youth', in which children and adolescents mourned the assassination by sitting together and lighting candles in the streets, posed new challenges to counsellors. How to react to it? How should teachers relate to it? How should the school address the opposing views of students which are expressed in various actions?

When, for example, two girls from one of the orthodox schools in the south of the country recently supported the murderer of the former Israeli Prime Minister and wrote him letters of support, the counsellor in that school was expected to intervene. The counsellor indeed met with the girls, the families and the classmates. Is this the role of the counsellor? Was the the girls' action part of the school climate or was it connected with their personalities or home environment?

The peace process, a very controversial issue in Israel, is part of the daily life in the country. What is the role of the counsellor in this issue? Can he or she avoid relating to it? What about unusual reactions of students, and how they should be handled? This is a unique situation, but it shows the unusual factors of the social context that affect counselling and supervision.

Fourth, cutbacks in education pose a particular difficulty in counselling and supervision. Budget cuts usually affect supplementary services such as counselling. There is a desire on the part of the counsellor to satisfy and respond to every request in order to justify the role and the existence of a school counsellor. Counselors are often involved in tasks that are not part of their job description. Boundaries are not always clear – a difficulty which affects the work of both the counsellor and the supervisor.

Finally, the institution is an influencing contextual factor. The work of the counsellor in a school setting raises some problems. There is sometimes an ambiguity of roles. Questions often asked are: What is the role of the teacher in the school versus the counsellor in relation to the student? How does the relationship of the counsellor with other professionals in the school interfere with his or her counselling of the individual student? How does the principal's role affect the work of the counsellor? Is the fact that the principal is the evaluator and the head of the institution a factor in the counselling process of the counsellor? What is the relationship of the principal with the counselling supervisor? In times of budget cuts, when the principal can decide whether or not to have a school counsellor, how does it affect the work of the counsellor? How does it affect supervision?

In spite of these difficulties, we feel that counselling has a major impact in the school system. It can be attributed to the supervision network established from the first years of counselling in Israel and its dynamic, changing nature.

The professional development of the counsellor and respective supervisory modalities

In an integrated development model of supervision Stoltenberg (1993), referring to counselling students, tried to describe the developmental levels of the trainee in different domains and the supervision intervention given at different stages. Developmental models of individual supervision that have appeared in the counselling psychology literature include those by Litterell et al. (1979), Loganbill et al. (1982) and Blocher (1983). The models focus on the supervisor. Holloway (1987, 1988), in reviewing these models, comments on the problems in the methodology of these studies, due mostly to lack of longitudinal data and caution in drawing conclusions.

Since in Israel we have the experience of working with counsellors on the job and following their development, I do believe that at different stages of their professional development counsellors will benefit from different supervisory interventions (Skovholt and Ronnestad 1992). It is necessary, therefore, to identify the major stages in the professional development of the counsellor.

Stage theories of human development rely on sequences of stages that individuals pass through. The work of a given stage must be completed before the individual can progress to a higher level. The theoretical basis for the stages in the professional development of the counsellor as defined here was based on the developmental models used in vocational counselling such as those of Super et al. (1981). In order to test the applicability of these theories to the professional work of the counsellor in Israel, I met with groups of counsellors at different stages of their professional development and asked them to characterize the stage at which they felt they currently were.

Basic assumptions

There were some agreed basic assumptions which formed the basis for this model of professional development:

1. The professional development of the counsellor in the field is such that he or she may cycle and recycle through these various stages at different depth levels (Loganbill et al. 1982; Super et al. 1981). Each stage involves the fulfiling of relevant developmental tasks for that stage but the development is not necessarily linear.

2. Various factors can affect the rate of professional development of the counsellor – for example, educational experiences (working as a teacher) prior to work as a counsellor, other professional experiences, life experiences, work environment, and external rewards or intrinsic factors such as motivation

and self-exploration. The impact of supervision as an enhancer of the professional development of the school counsellor is emphasized by Henderson and Lampe (1992).

3. Concepts such as reflectivity (Neufeldt et al. 1996; Skovholdt and Ronnestad 1992), conceptualization (Stoltenberg 1981; Holloway 1987), autonomy (McNeill et al. 1985; Stoltenberg 1993), initiative and creativity are core concepts in the professional development of the counsellor and they change over time.

The following stages in the professional development of the counsellor in Israel were identified and characterized by the counsellors themselves. This identification was necessary in order to structure more systematic supervisory interventions that would help the counsellor to progress successfully from one level to the next. Supervisory modes are recommended for each stage. Supervision in the early stages of the counsellor's development is mandatory. At later stages it is more negotiable and varies according to the needs and style of the main counselling supervisor.

Stages in professional development

FANTASY   The novice counsellor comes with unrealistic expectations and an unclear vision of the profession. Some school counsellors were formerly teachers and have difficulties in changing into the new role. Some made a compromise by taking counselling instead of a more prestigious subject (such as clinical psychology, etc.). At this early stage the novice counsellor is influenced by these factors and by the hazy picture he or she has of the profession. Most of them say that the transition from an academic environment to practical work as a counsellor is very hard and they feel unprepared. This is largely due to the dynamic social and political life in Israel and its demands on this profession.

At this stage individual supervision by a senior counsellor-supervisor is necessary to facilitate the transition from academia to work, to clarify realistic expectations and to set goals. In addition, group meetings with the general supervisor appointed by the Ministry of Education are held in order to familiarize the counsellor with his or her role and with various procedures related to the work.

EXPLORATION OF THE PROFESSION   This is the second identified stage. It involves, first, trying out the various roles of the counsellor as described above, but in particular counselling, consultation and co-ordination of work with others (team work). There is less involvement in organizational consultation, planning and evaluation. The counsellor at this stage is less autonomous, less initiating and tries to respond to the demands of the system, instead of planning ahead. The counsellor bases his or her work mostly on theory and needs help in applying conceptual principles to the tasks of counselling. At this stage supervision continues on a one-to-one basis, with emphasis on planning and counselling skills. In addition, the counsellor benefits from the 'specialist' supervisor, getting help and familiarizing him or herself with various counselling programmes. Group consultation meetings organized by the general supervisor are also ongoing.

CRYSTALLIZING PROFESSIONAL IDENTITY   At this stage the counsellor clarifies roles, evaluating him- or herself in a more realistic manner, with the professional expectations of self and others becoming clearer. The counsellor is aware of limits, of possible role conflicts and of counselling processes, is more initiating and combines knowledge with affective processes. He or she can plan and develop a developmental counselling programme. At this stage the counsellor benefits most from group supervision. This is given by the senior counsellor in a setting of a small group of counsellors. The counsellor also continues to get help in programme development from the 'specialist' supervisors.

IMPLEMENTING PROFESSIONAL IDENTITY   The counsellor can implement the various skills acquired and apply them to more complex counselling situations. The counsellor is aware of ethical and moral dilemmas and can use professional judgement in complex counselling situations more effectively. This is the stage at which peer supervision, where counsellors consult on more complex cases, can be useful. Also, in-service workshops in ethical dilemmas or special counselling interventions are taking place, usually organized by the general supervisor.

STABILIZATION AND SPECIALIZATION   At this stage the counsellor feels more confident in the role of counsellor and in the various domains of work. He or she expresses a preference for certain areas of work and implements knowledge and skills in this area. The counsellor specializes in a certain area, usually in an academic environment, while using his or her expertise in the work. At this stage counsellors are involved in some type of supervisory or specialization training qualifying them to function as specialists in one of the areas of counselling. Successful counsellors at this stage serve as trainers for university students in counselling.

ADVANCEMENT   The counsellor is usually promoted to a role of a 'specialist' or a senior counsellor-supervisor. He or she acquires supervision skills in addition to their particular specialization and implements them in individual and group supervision. This is the stage at which the counsellor is engaged formally in the roles of specialist and counsellor-supervisor and thus is accountable for his or her supervisory role to one of the people in the department (Sheffy). In addition, the counsellor is involved in the development of evaluation and research plans.

RENEWAL   At this stage the counsellor feels a need for renewal either by pursuing further education, choosing a different direction or retiring.

At each stage of the counsellor's development, the supervisor appointed by the Ministry of Education has to assess which interventions could be most appropriate in order to develop the required competencies of the counsellor and promote accountability of counselling. At times he/she undertakes the supervision; alternatively, others are appointed to perform the appropriate interventions. This model also denotes at which stage the counsellor is ready to become a supervisor or a specialist.

One of the tools that can be useful in achieving the goals of supervision and in helping to follow closely and developmentally the work of the counsellor, is the portfolio. Portfolios are an alternative assessment method that have been used extensively in the evaluation of professionals and students in various academic areas (Wolf 1991). They are defined as a collection of evidence documenting an individual's development competencies and quality (Waterman 1991). Portfolios were found useful in particular with counsellors because of their structured and developmental nature.

There follows a description of a supervision case by Aliza, a counsellor-supervisor who was requested as part of her training as a supervisor to provide supervision to a beginning counsellor and write it up in a portfolio.

Supervision case

Aliza has worked as a counsellor for fourteen years, has supervised counsellors informally for the last year, and has just finished her graduate studies. She is forty-two years old and is taking a university course, training to become a supervisor. She describes her work with the supervisee, a young novice counsellor who has just started work.

The counsellor is described in relation to her level of experience in the role, her theoretical orientation, learning needs, cultural characteristics and self presentation (Holloway 1995). The reaction of the supervisor at this point was in relation to the educational level of the supervisee (counsellor). Both had an MA in counselling, but while the supervisee was young and had finished it fast, the supervisor had difficulties in doing so. This became a contextual factor which affected the supervisory relationship at the beginning. The supervisee wanted supervision in particular in relation to the many expectations she faced in her school. She needed to sort out these expectations and decide what it was realistic for her to fulfil. The supervisor identified this as the first stage in the counsellor's professional development (as described earlier) and intervened accordingly. In addition, the supervisor reflected on the importance that the counsellor gave to the institution – the school – as a significant contextual factor. One of the problems encountered at this stage by the supervisee was her desire to satisfy the demands of the teachers at the school, who tended to refer a lot of students to her, hoping she could find an immediate solution to their problems, thus justifying her role as a school counsellor. The supervisor reflected on the parallel process at this stage. Her own need to satisfy the supervisee and respond immediately to her requests in this way would justify her position as a supervisor.

The specific sessions were analysed in the portfolio according to the tasks and functions of supervision, following Holloway's model (1995), with the supervisor's reflection and the feedback she got from her peer supervisors when presenting the sessions in class. One of the cases the counsellor (supervisee) brought up in supervision was the killing of the brother of one of the students in school in an army attack. The counsellor was involved in consulting the teachers about the case and talking to the students in the class. In the supervision session she mostly wanted instructions as to what to do with the teachers and what to say in the classroom. Because of the many crisis situations in Israel, there are specific guidelines as to what to do in such situations. Nevertheless, in this case the counsellor felt at a loss. Aliza, the supervisor, reflected on the fact that in the process of supervision at this point, she was mostly involved in consulting and instructing around the professional role of the counsellor and giving instructions, while she really felt she should have been involved in supporting and sharing. It was surprising to her that the counsellor was focused on the procedural aspects of the crisis, because crisis intervention in Israel is one of the major areas of counselling and supervision. Policy and procedures for the supervision network response in Israel are outlined in the next section.

Crisis intervention procedure and the role of supervision

The Department of Counseling and Psychological Services has prepared written procedures for crisis events (Klingman 1997). These procedures are used nationally and locally, for example in times of war (such as the Gulf War), terrorist attacks (bombing of buses and cafés in Jerusalem, Tel Aviv and other areas), bombing of northern cities by the Lebanese army; and, on a smaller scale, in cases of fatal car accidents, murder, death or other disasters. Every school district has a crisis team which includes the counselling supervisor, the general school supervisor, the expert supervisor if necessary and the district psychologist and which acts as a consulting team to the district manager in a crisis situation.

On a smaller scale, each school has to have a crisis team, headed by the principal of the school, and co-ordinated by the counsellor. The task of the team is to prepare the school for crisis situations. The team organizes simulations for the teachers and students, collects materials and designs specific programmes to deal with crisis situations. In the case of a real emergency, the team convenes at once and decides on the plan of action. Usually all the teachers are immediately convened by the team and are given instructions on how to deal with the students in the classroom and students who need special attention and care. The team is responsible for giving out accurate information to students, teachers and parents and planning the activities in the school, such as work in the classroom, work in groups and with individual students. The team is helped by other professionals outside the area (if it is not a national disaster), such as counselling supervisors and senior counsellor-supervisors. The counselling supervisor of the school district or the specific school has to be immediately notified of the disaster and acts as a consultant to the team. The counselling supervisor consults if necessary with the head of counselling in the Ministry of Education. The head of counselling, in the event of a major crisis, updates the Minister of Education.

Summary and recommendations

The network of supervisors in Israel as described here is possible mainly because of the allocation of a budget for this purpose. The professional supervision given to school counsellors by the counselling supervisor, helped by the senior counsellor and the specialist, is an important contribution to the professional development of the counsellor in each school and to the profession of counselling in general. It also provides a route of advancement for the counsellor.

There is a need to structure even further the supervision given to the counsellors at each stage of their development and according to their specific needs. Because of variations in school districts and in needs in different areas of the country, there are still differences in the supervisory modalities. On the other hand, because it is all centred in the Department of Counselling and Psychological Services of the Ministry of Education, and there is a uniform definition of counselling policy, supervisors can work in a systematic and organized manner. At the same time, autonomy of the supervisor is still possible. It is important to keep this balance between a policy of supervision that will enable individual differences but at the same time will answer organizational and regional needs.

References

ACES (Association for Counselor Education and Supervision) (1995) 'Ethical guidelines for counseling supervisors', *Counselor Education and Supervision*, 34: 270–6.

Barret, R.L. and Schmidt, J.J. (1986) 'School counselor certification and supervision: overlooked professional issues', *Counselor Education and Supervision*, 26: 50–5.

Benshoff, J.M. and Paisley, P.O. (1996) 'The structured peer consultation model for school counselors', *Journal of Counseling and Development*, 74: 314–18.

Bernstein, B.L., Forrest, L. and Golston, S.S. (1994) 'Current practices of counseling psychology faculty in K-12 schools: a national survey', *The Counseling Psychologist*, 22: 611–27.

Blocher, D.H. (1983) 'Toward a cognitive developmental approach to counseling supervision', *The Counseling Psychologist*, 11: 27–34.

Borders, L.D. and Schmidt, J.J. (1992) 'Innovative approaches to the professional development of school counselors', *The School Counselor*, 39: 148–50.

Borders, L.D. and Usher, C.H. (1992) 'Post-degree supervision: existing and preferred practices', *Journal of Counseling and Development*, 70: 594–7.

Boyd, J. (1987) *Counselor supervision*. Muncie, IN: Accelerated Development.

Campbell, C.A. (1992) 'The school counselor as consultant: assessing your aptitude', *Elementary School and Guidance Counseling*, 26: 237–50.

Crutchfield, L.B. and Borders, L.D. (1997) 'Impact of two clinical peer supervision models on practicing school counselors', *Journal of Counseling and Development*, 75: 219–30.

Henderson, P. and Lampe, R.E. (1992) 'Clinical supervision of school counselors', *The School Counselor*, 39: 151–7.

Holloway, E.L. (1987) 'Developmental models of supervision: is it development?' *Professional Psychology: Research and Practice*, 18: 209–16.

Holloway, E.L. (1988) 'Models of counselor development or training models for supervision: rejoinder to Stoltenberg and Delworth', *Professional Psychology: Research and Practice*, 19: 138–40.

Holloway, E.L. (1995) *Clinical Supervision: A Systems Approach*. Thousand Oaks, CA: Sage.

Klingman, A. (1997) *Coping with Crises in Schools: Emergency Kit*. Jerusalem: Publications Department, Ministry of Education.

Litterell, J.M., Lee-Borden, N. and Lorenz, J. (1979) 'Developmental framework for counseling supervision', *Counselor Education and Supervision*, 19: 129–36.

Loganbill, C., Hardy, E. and Delworth, U. (1982) 'Supervision: a conceptual model', *The Counseling Psychologist*, 10: 3–42.

McNeill, B.W. and Stoltenberg, C.D. (1992) 'Agendas for developmental supervision research: a response to Borders', *Counselor Education and Supervision*, 31: 179–83.

McNeill, B.W., Stoltenberg, C.D. and Pierce, D.A. (1985) 'Supervisees' perceptions of their development: a test of the counselor complexity model', *Journal of Counseling Psychology*, 32: 630–3.

Neufeldt, S.A., Karno, M.P. and Nelson, M.L. (1996) 'A qualitative study of experts' conceptualizations of supervisee reflectivity', *Journal of Counseling Psychology*, 43: 1, 3–9.

Roberts, E.B. and Borders, L.D. (1994) 'Supervision of school counselors: administrative, program and counseling', *The School Counselor*, 41: 149–57.

Schmidt, J.J. (1990) 'Critical issues for school counselor performance, appraisal and supervision', *The School Counselor*, 38: 86–94.

Skovholt, T.M. and Ronnestad, M.H. (1992) *'The evolving professional self: stages and themes in therapist and counselor development'*, Chichester: Wiley.

Stoltenberg, C. (1981) 'Approaching supervision from a developmental perspective: the counselor complexity model', *Journal of Counseling Psychology*, 28: 59–65.

Stoltenberg, C. (1993) 'Supervising consultants in training: an application of a model of supervision', *Journal of Counseling and Development*, 72: 131–8.

Stoltenberg, C. and Delworth, U. (1988) 'Developmental models of supervision: it is development. A response to Holloway', *Professional Psychology: Research and Practice*, 19: 134–7.

Super, D.E., Thompson, A.S., Lindeman, R.H., Jordaan, J.P. and Myers, R.A. (1981) *Career Development Inventory*. Palo Alto, CA: Consulting Psychologists Press.

Waterman, M.A. (1991) 'Teaching portfolios for summative and peer evaluation'. Paper presented at the Sixth American Association for Higher Education Conference on Assessment for Higher Education, San Francisco.

Wolf, K.P. (1991) *Teaching Portfolios: A Synthesis of Research and Annotated Bibliography*. San Francisco: Far West Laboratories.

8 Supervision in workplace settings

Michael Carroll

Within the supervisory literature, and indeed within supervisory practice, there is some debate and disagreement around what should and should not be included in supervision proper. These areas include clear demarcation between personal therapy and supervision, the role of evaluation and supervisee assessment within supervision and the teaching/learning methods adopted by supervisors which are wide and often differing. A fourth area of some contention is whether or not supervision ought to deal with the organizational dimension of client work or concentrate solely on individual clients. While some of these unagreed arenas are due to the youthfulness of the supervision profession, others can be traced to the counselling orientation of the supervisor (Carroll 1995).

It is in the area of workplace counselling that many of these conflicts converge, not necessarily because they are supervisory conflicts *per se* but because workplace counselling, as a counselling modality, is still very unclear in its role and purpose (Carroll 1997a). By and large, workplace counselling models are adapted from traditional counselling approaches (Bull 1997; Carroll 1996b) and to date we do not have a model of counselling in the workplace in its own right. Both training and supervision have based themselves on this principle because private practice is still the ideal of the counselling world. This has resulted in some difficulty for counsellors in the workplace faced with an array of issues not confronted by counsellors in other contexts, particularly the context of private practice. There is increasing awareness that working with the organization becomes a central focus in the life of workplace counsellors and requests for further involvement in organizational change and transition are made continually. C. Carroll's research into employee counsellors' perspectives on their tasks and roles (1997) has revealed how counsellors, usually trained in the traditional modes and orientations, have found difficulty in adapting their counselling to the workplace. She isolates the features of workplace counsellors as: multi-skilled, that is, able to move easily between a number of roles; flexible, that is, adaptable to the demands and exigencies of the organization; and competent to work in the organization as well as with the individual client. Not only do employee counsellors work with individual clients but they are being asked more and more to make a contribution to organizational change (Walton 1997a). However, recent research into workplace counselling has shown it to be an effective individual intervention but one that hardly touches the organization itself. Berridge, Cooper and Highley-Marchington (1997: 168, 174) draw the following conclusions from their study of workplace counselling:

> After receiving counselling (and at follow-up) clients reported significantly improved mental well-being compared with before counselling. . . . The introduction of an Employee Assistance Programme does affect the individual being counselled, but not the whole employee population, in terms of mental and physical health, job satisfaction and sources of pressure.

For many employers this is not satisfactory. Clearly, they want counselling to work with their individual employees, especially those in crisis, but they also want counselling and a counselling philosophy to impact the organization as a whole (Carroll 1997b; Walton 1997a).

This chapter looks in some detail at supervision in workplace counselling. There is very little experience and less agreement on the salient features of supervision in this area. Questions raised for supervisors who would venture into this area are:

- How far does supervision deal with the organizational and contextual issues emerging from client work?
- Can supervision provide a forum for counsellors to look at their roles and responsibilities, other than individual counselling work, within a workplace setting?
- What issues emerge for employee counsellors and how far are these valid focus-points for supervision, for example, politics within the organization, line-management issues, training, consultancy to senior management?

It is my contention that supervision of counsellors *must* deal with whatever affects client work, either directly or indirectly, and in these circumstances of the workplace, I am convinced that the organization in which counselling takes place has a vast impact on counsellors, clients and the counselling provision.

Counselling in the workplace

Perhaps a word on issues pertinent to workplace counselling will contextualize the discussion before concentrating on supervision. Counselling has taken some time to find a niche within the workplace: the two worlds of counselling and business have found historical difficulties in relating constructively to one another. There are several reasons for this poor relationship. First of all, and mentioned briefly above, from its beginnings counselling and counsellors, presumably from its roots in Freud, have adopted private practice as their ideal. As such, training in counselling has concentrated on the individual aspects of the work with clients: the therapeutic relationship, the skills needed to work with clients, the confidentiality that is part of the therapeutic relationship, and even the blocks and unfinished issues within counsellors that could affect the outcome. Rarely, in traditional counselling training, were students taught how to understand and work with the administrative and organizational aspects of counselling: how to set up a counselling service, how to manage the various aspects of counselling provision, how to integrate counselling into an existing organization, how to negotiate and educate organizations to understand and value counselling interventions, how to use counselling as a form of organizational change. It is only when counsellors began the journey from private, individual work to working within companies that questions about their roles and relationships to the organization began to emerge. Two recent books trace some of the issues and difficulties experienced by clinicians when they move from the private arena into working with organizations. One of these entitled *From Couch to Corporation* (Martin 1996), brings the counsellor through what it calls 'Your couch-to-corporation transformation', outlining the shifts needed to make the transition successfully. The second, *Corporate Therapy and Consulting* (Sperry 1996), undertakes to extend 'clinical skills to organizational settings' and outlines the skills of the corporate therapist as he or she begins to work with clinical-organizational interventions. Both, while lauding the skills brought by counsellors to companies, do not underestimate the difficulties clinicians have in moving into the industrial ambience.

The second reason why counselling and the workplace have been alien bedfellows is the fact that counsellors are uneasy when boundary issues are threatened. Industry has had a history of accountability: audits are part and parcel of organizational life and never more so than today with its emphasis on competitiveness, flatter organizations and downsizing as a way of reducing overheads. Industry, also, has a history of leakage in communication. Knowledge moves rapidly, both formally and informally, throughout the organization, and counsellors are often under extreme pressure to share information with line-managers, occupational health personnel, human resources/personnel departments. This has resulted in counsellors working in companies as if they were doing private practice, or indeed with some counsellors seeing themselves on the side of the individual client *against* the organization. They take on the role of a single-handed union battling against the alien forces of management to protect the victim, the individual employee. I have heard workplace counsellors berate their organizations, the management systems involved, the policies, the treatment of individuals, and heard them talk about intervening in the organization in ways which indicate they, the counsellors are 'at war' with it, the company, over individual rights.

One of the major skills, for both workplace counsellors and their supervisors, is the ability to hold in tension and in some relief polarities that emerge from:

- the needs of the individual versus the needs of the organization;
- the values of counselling versus the values of business;
- the role of counselling versus taking on other roles;
- the need to look after individuals and the needs of groups.

Supervising workplace counsellors

This chapter will outline 11 focus-points for supervisors as they engage in supervision with individual counsellors or counselling teams within the workplace. These 11 points (Carroll 1996b; Proctor 1997b) are factors over and above the clear central purpose of supervision which is around the welfare of clients and the quality of the work with them. This chapter presumes that supervisors of workplace counsellors will have client-work at the centre of their gaze. There are a number of excellent texts outlining how supervisors work with individual clients irrespective of the context (Bernard and Goodyear 1992; Carroll 1996a; Hawkins and Shohet 1989; Holloway 1995; Inskipp and Proctor 1993, 1995; Page and Wosket 1994). These 11 points subsume the centrality of the client and the quality of the individual work as essential and add additional areas requiring consideration for workplace counsellors. Additional here does not mean other than work with clients, but additional areas that affect that work. The 11 organizational tasks of supervising workplace counsellors are to:

1. Generate clear contracts with all parties.
2. Enable counsellors to work and live within organizations.
3. Help counsellors control the flow of information.
4. Help counsellors manage the counselling provision.
5. Work with counsellors at the interface between the individual and the organization.
6. Help counsellors look after and support themselves as they work within organizations.
7. Where appropriate, work with a team of employee counsellors.
8. Facilitate counsellors in the management of records, statistics, reports and the communication of these to the organization.
9. Work with counsellors to understand and manage the parallel process within organizations.
10. Help counsellors build working models for understanding counselling within organizations.
11. Evaluate, with counsellors, how counselling can be a vehicle for understanding and facilitating organizational change and transition.

Each of these tasks will be considered in turn.

1. Generate clear contracts with all parties

There are a number of ways in which supervisors are contracted to work with counsellors in the workplace (Carroll 1996a: Chapter 10). Some supervisors are hired by the counsellor/s and paid by them independently. Others are chosen by the counsellor/s and paid by the organization. Rarely, if ever, do organizations ask supervisors they pay to have more than a financial contract with them. Usually, they are quite happy to trust both counsellor and supervisor to get on with the job and they pay the bill accordingly. As a result, supervisors gauge their roles and responsibilities alone and without discussion with anyone in the organization. This is a pity, because supervisors need to work with the organization to clarify:

- their responsibility to the organization: when they might intervene in the organization with or without the permission of the counsellor;
- what feedback they give to the organization regarding the counselling service and the counsellors (for example, supervisory reports which can be used in annual appraisal);
- what areas they will work on with the counsellor and when this might involve organizational issues;
- what kind of confidentiality pertains and when it might be reasonable to expect a supervisor to take the Official Secrets Act (for example, a supervisor of a counsellor working in the Foreign Office might need to be aware of this).

Contracts clarify roles and responsibilities, they outline expectations from all parties, and they eliminate, to some degree, the process of game-playing. The contract, above all, minimizes surprises and ensures that all parties have thought through, before the work begins, their responsibilities and obligations to one another and to the organization. In a chapter entitled 'Contracts in supervision' Brigid Proctor (1997a: 196) applies this to employee counselling services and writes:

> any supervisor working for them [employee counselling services] may want to decide if any duty they or their supervisee is expected to undertake contravenes any professional values, and to contract (about e.g., boundaries of confidentiality or practice expectations) either at the outset or when clashes become clear as the work proceeds.

My suggestion is that a formal contract, hopefully before the supervisory work begins, allows and rehearses for possibilities in conflicts of roles, expectations and responsibilities. It is always possible to return to the contract and re-negotiate what has not been covered or what is not working as it was expected.

2. Enable counsellors to work and live within organizations

Workplace counsellors are often asked to fulfil a number of roles within organizations: counsellor, trainer, consultant, adviser, publicist, advocate, policy maker. It is important that they have a forum, supervision, where they can look at possible role-conflict. I remember a manager phoning a counsellor to ask if she would tell her client, a member of his department, that he, the client, was about to be made redundant in the new round of downsizing. Clearly, the manager was offloading his task on to her but with the good reason that she had an excellent relationship with the client while his was not so good. This was a clear example of role-conflict had the counsellor taken on the task and could have both damaged the therapeutic relationship with the client as well as absolved the organization from assuming its responsibly to its employees.

To whom is the counsellor responsible in line-management terms and what information should he/she share with others about individual clients? Often counsellors are part of occupational health departments where decisions have to be made about continuing employment where counsellors are working with an employee who is sick. I was asked recently by the Head of Human Resources to consult with him about a client from the company whom I was seeing for counselling. The Human Resources Manager did not want to know about the counselling, simply if, in my professional judgement, the client was strong enough to hear the news that she was being released by the organization. Is it part of my role to provide that consultation? Ought a counsellor provide a professional opinion to an organization that could result in what clients might perceive as negative news, for example being made redundant? Counselling could then be used as a way of 'fattening up' employees so that they are psychologically strong enough to hear 'bad news'.

Changing relationships are part and parcel of the lives of workplace counsellors: the individual on the stress-management course wants to come for personal counselling, the manager on the subcommittee on harassment at work approaches the counsellor with personal issues, there are even instances of line-managers coming to the counselling service with personal problems. Supervisors offer the forum where counsellors can look in more detail at their roles and possible clashes and confusions around them. However, without a clear contract to understand the relationship between organization and counsellor the supervisor may not be able to guide counsellors towards effective problem-solving in this area.

3. Help counsellors control the flow of information

Egan (1994) has highlighted the importance of the 'shadow-side' of organizations – that informal network of relationships and communication which exists in all companies. It is here that confidential information often finds a route through the system. Counsellors have to ask: Who shares what information with whom? This can be quite a tricky situation, with line-managers looking for information (often to help employees); disciplinary and health boards, and even lawyers in some instances, asking counsellors for their opinions, and occasionally even clients asking counsellors to act on their behalf with the organization or groups within it. The other side is also true, with the counsellor occasionally being the recipient of information that may not be used with the client: for example, the manager who offers information about the client that the client has not shared with the counsellor. Supervision provides the context in which counsellors can reflect on the appropriateness of where they share what they know, and how they educate the system to give them information they can use with clients. And, on the other hand, counsellors use supervision to reflect on how they can feed back information into the system without jeopardizing individual client confidentiality. Walton (1997a) has listed a number of areas around this situation, especially when counsellors provide feedback to the company.

4. Help counsellors manage the counselling provision

In many instances, workplace counsellors not only provide counselling but have to manage the counselling service with all that means administratively, financially and integratively. This management function of counsellors is not one they are trained to do as part of counselling training and they may well need help from supervisors in how to integrate and administer the service in a professional organization. Recently two of my supervisees (both in-house workplace counsellors) were asked by their organizations to set up an evaluation process for their counselling services. Not having done it before, and wanting to provide the best audit, both brought this to supervision where we spent some time in reviewing an approach. Another supervisee was asked by her line-manager to write a brochure for employees about the counselling service; another, again, to make a presentation to the Board of Directors (given 20 minutes) on how he saw the counselling service as 'adding value' to the company. Workplace counsellors may be requested to provide a budget for the forthcoming year, to review resources needed (space facilities, secretarial resources), to do appraisal interviews and even be skilled in performance management with 'direct reports', for example other counsellors and office support workers. Supervisors need to be aware of these issues as essential to contemporary organizations and be able to understand and help counsellors find help with their other responsibilities. Most workplace counsellors are also managers of their services. It brings up the issue of supervisors having specialized skills and knowledge in areas not demanded of them in other contexts, for example private practice.

5. Work with counsellors at the interface between the individual and the organization

Organizations are, to some extent, like individuals and families: they have their own personality or what is called 'culture' (Lane 1990; Hawkins and Shohet 1989; Walton 1997b). Organizational culture expresses that indefinable something that characterizes a particular company, gives it its own special flavour and to a large degree determines how employees relate to one another and behave towards the organization. It is crucial that all employees – and workplace counsellors are employees – learn to understand the culture of the company. In understanding it they will learn how to communicate, how to affect and influence, who to approach about what, and what are the critical points within the organization that are very sensitive. This understanding and 'being-part-of' has both advantages and disadvantages for employee counsellors. On the one hand they are part and parcel of the culture and can work with it; on the other hand, they are so close to it and immersed in it (after a while) that they may not see the dysfunctional elements involved. It is here that external supervision can be of assistance in helping employee counsellors get the distance they need to make decisions about how to work with this particular culture and how to work at the interface between individual client and organization. One team of work-place counsellors I supervised were continually frustrated with their efforts to give feedback to management on practices causing problems within the organization. It was only in working with them to understand the power and bureaucratic elements within the company that the team gained insights into how threatening was their feedback to management who felt they were being reproached for the ills of the organization. Finding alternative ways of reporting and alternative methods was less frustrating. Supervisors provide an 'objective' view often lacking to those caught up in the day-to-day functioning of the organization.

6. Help counsellors look after and support themselves as they work within organizations

Most workplace counsellors find it difficult to manage their time effectively with heavy case-loads as well as fulfilling all the other jobs that come their way, for example group work, publicity, keeping records, liaising with management, training, not to mention emergencies, etc. Hawkins and Shohet (1989) have used the term 'bucket-theory' to illustrate how workplace counsellors end up carrying the problems, distresses and difficulties of the organization, almost as if employees dump them in the counselling room. Furthermore, expectations from the organization and from the counsellors themselves can add further stress, especially in the beginning when the counselling service is trying to prove itself and gain credence within the organization.

Supervision offers an oasis for workplace counsellors where they can review what is happening to them, and their personal and professional lives, while at the same time regaining both energy and rationalization in their commitments. It is also a place where counsellors can think about and receive guidance on further training to meet the issues emerging for them.

7. Where appropriate, work with a team of employee counsellors

More and more organizations engage full teams of counsellors or EAPs that have groups of associates. Supervising the workplace counselling team brings its own set of dynamics over and above supervising individual counsellors. More writing is needed urgently on group supervision and even more so on group team supervision, that is, where the group is an existing team. Focus-points within this work will be the role of the team within the organization and the relationships and dynamics within the team itself that contribute to the counselling work. Inskipp and Proctor (1995) point out the dual tasks of group supervision as being 'supervising the individuals with regard to client and supervisee needs and harnessing the individuals into an effective learning and working group'. In staff team supervision the second of these will often become predominant; in fact, in many ways the quality of the client work will depend on the cohesiveness of the staff team. There are several points on which supervision can concentrate, besides individual client work:

- the team as group
- the relationship of the team to the supervisor
- the team within the organization.

The supervisor who works with employee counselling teams needs to have, besides supervisory skills, some understanding of groups, group processes and intergroup processes.

8. Facilitate counsellors in the management of records, statistics, reports and the communication of these to the organization

Workplace counsellors are required, almost without exception, to keep records of their work, counselling and otherwise, and furnish annual reports to the company. In their simplest form these reports will outline statistics on who has used the service, the general problems brought and how these numbers relate to over-all numbers within the company. In some instances these reports are used to argue for continuation of the service and/or for funding or increase of the service. They are vitally important, especially today when companies are aware of cost-cutting and evaluating value for money. Most likely, someone in the company will ask if the counselling service provides value for money. Reports and statistics, as well as evaluation procedures and audits, can help counsellors argue their points, especially if these reports are well done and well presented.

This is another area where supervision can help. Many counsellors have no background in gathering data, in analysing it and in reporting it comprehensively. And indeed, many supervisors do not possess such knowledge and skills. Awareness that organizations may require the maintaining of statistics and provision of reports at least allows supervisors and workplace counsellors to consider where effective help can be sought, if not in supervision, to offer the appropriate support.

9. Work with counsellors to understand and manage the parallel process within organizations

Parallel process can be seen in the image of a 'hot potato' that is passed along institutional lines and even departments without anyone stopping to evaluate where it really belongs and where it should be solved. So individuals are scapegoated within departments (the individual is made to take responsibility for the 'hot potato' while the department denies it exists); or individuals will take on roles within the group or the organization that save the others from having to express them. Parallel process means that one part of the organization will reflect what is happening in another. So the counselling service can become the 'human face of the organization' (C. Carroll 1997) which relieves the rest of the organization from having to show compassion, to listen, to nurture and to show concern. The term 'institutional transference' has been used to show how people will transfer on to the organization issues that are personal to them (authority issues, paranoid problems, etc.) and vice versa, the organization will transfer on to individuals issues it, the organization, is not dealing with or wants to deal with, for example low morale, depression, etc. Workplace counsellors have to assess situations in the light of what belongs to the individual client and what belongs to the organization and find ways of locating the source of problems rather than simply where it is expressed.

Supervision, in its turn, becomes a further extension of the organization where again parallel issues are expressed. Workplace counsellors will do to their supervisor what the organization has done to them. Effective supervisors pick this up and work with it rather than take it personally or blame the counsellor. Understanding and working with individual and organizational transference issues becomes a key element in supervision.

10. Help counsellors build working models for understanding counselling within organizations

Workplace counsellors bring with them, from other settings, counselling models that they adapt, or not, to the workplace. C.

Carroll's research (1997) has shown that many feel guilty as they learn how to work with clients in a multi-roled manner and feel that their 'purist' roots are being sullied as they make the needs of clients the springboard for their interventions rather than their theories. Where supervisors can help is in allowing them to use their experience to build working models of workplace counselling that combine professionalism and ethical parameters with clear responses to the needs of their client group. It may well be that 'sacred cows' from counselling training (for example the 50-minute session, seeing clients once a week, using the same room for clients) make no sense in this context. Indeed, why should they? Should counselling be denied an executive who spends most of his life in aeroplanes and can attend for a morning every month? Can effective counselling take place for three hours once a month where the counsellor meets the client in London, Paris, New York? Models of workplace counselling may well build in three-way meetings as a helpful element in the work: meetings between the individual client, the counsellor and another party, whether that be a line-manager, Human Resources Director, a team or a Department, a union member, whatever. Working models for workplace counselling will look at brief therapy but be able to think in long-term ways, will think psychiatrically and medically as well as intra-psychically, and will connect client problems to company policies. Supervisors, and workplace counsellors, need to be aware of the changing nature of the counselling contract within organizations and be prepared to re-negotiate what is needed by the individual client and the organization.

11. Evaluate, with counsellors, how counselling can be a vehicle for understanding and facilitating organizational change and transition

As more and more companies evaluate their counselling services they may well feel that they want more organizational value for their money as well as the individual value they receive at present. Perhaps it is time for workplace counsellors, and their supervisors, to begin to think of how counselling philosophy, methods, and applications can relate to and help the wider organization without endangering the valuable work it does with individual clients. Carroll (Lecture at the University of Utrecht,

The Netherlands, April, 1997) has outlined several ways in which this could happen:

- By providing insights into organizations. Different counselling traditions can offer organization insights, for example, the psychodynamic concept of organizations (defences, transference, unconscious elements), the shadow-side of organizations (Egan 1994). Systemic understandings of organizations can be helpful here, for example the inter-relatedness of change systems. Other counselling orientations can be equally valuable here, such as use of the Gestalt cycle of "stuckness" (Critchley and Casey 1989) and the person-centred approaches to leadership and management.
- By providing individual interventions that combine counselling roles and skills with other forms of relationships, for example, one-to-one executive coaching, mentoring systems, supervision and consultancy to managers and teams.
- By providing organizational interventions such as a philosophy of employee care, systems of employee well-being, policies and statements about employee rights and responsibilities (for example sexual harassment, equal opportunities) as well as a commitment to an organizational culture of excellence based on people.

These insights, knowledge and skills work out in five systems that can help organizations move and develop:

1. individual crisis interventions
2. individual developmental issues systems
3. group developmental growth
4. training and development throughout the learning organization
5. organizational change and transition as needed.

And for supervisors and workplace counsellors it means new mindsets as they think differently in order to act differently. These mindset changes revolve around a movement between areas as outlined below:

> From individual thinking to organizational thinking.
> From individual assessment to assessment in a context.
> From interpersonal relationships to systems relations.
> From uni-role involvement to multi-role involvement.
> From being a counsellor to being a counselling consultant.
> From setting up counselling to integrating counselling into the workplace.

From personal accountability to organizational accountability.
From non-evaluation to evaluation.
From single intervention to organizational intervention.
From personal change to organizational change.

The skilled workplace counselling supervisor

Supervisors need to be skilled in many of these 11 tasks: not all are needed, and supervisees will come with requests to cover particular areas of these tasks. I supervise two counsellors specifically on the organizational aspects of their work – I have no contract with them to work with individual clients – they are supervised for that somewhere else. There may well be several areas of the 11 tasks above in which supervisors do not feel they have the experience or expertise to work with workplace counsellors. Nor should they try. What is more beneficial is that they recognize that these areas are valid areas for supervision and help supervisees find the help they need.

Supervisors require knowledge and skills in the following areas:

- knowledge of organizations and organizational culture;
- awareness of the dynamics that exist within organizations and the influences brought to bear on the counsellor and the counselling service by these dynamics;
- an ability to supervise across a number of professions: managers, Human Resources, personnel, supervision of supervisors, secretaries, etc.;
- work with people who want to spend time reviewing how the organization impacts on their lives (managers, etc.);
- counselling management and administration;
- work with varying roles and responsibilities.

Case study

Beatrice is the in-house counsellor for a company of approximately 2,500 employees. Her work consists of providing confidential individual counselling to employees for personal and professional problems. She is phoned by the Chief Executive Officer (CEO) who asks her to see Nigel, one of his managers (aged 52) who is taking early retirement on medical grounds. The CEO is aware that he, Nigel, is dealing with a number of personal issues and thinks counselling, before he leaves the company, might help him sort out some of them and put him in a stronger position to either get a new job or accept retirement. Beatrice, as is her policy, suggests that Nigel contact her for an appointment.

In the first session it becomes clear to Beatrice that Nigel has some quite deep-set relationship issues that seem to go back to early relationships with both parents. He is unable to form any kinds of close relationships, he can be aggressive and demanding and he has very little insight into his own issues. His marriage, which has been shaky for the past few years, is coming to an end and his wife has moved out of the family home. Their two children are grown up. He shares with Beatrice that he thinks no one in the company cares about him, he rubbishes the whole management set-up and then drops a bombshell. He has some papers that show up the company in a bad light and if published would, at least, be bad for publicity. He says that once his medical release is completed it is his intention to approach the national newspapers with his story. The published result will show what a lousy company this is and how badly it treats both its employees and its customers. Beatrice and Nigel agree to meet and work together until his release from the company (about three months' time).

In supervision, a decision is made that Beatrice will not do anything, at the moment, about Nigel's threats *vis-à-vis* the company but will work with him to see if they can deal with some of the immediate problems: his marriage break-up, a small financial debt, his inappropriateness in relationships with others and his retirement. If he can gain some insights into the patterns of his life, particularly around his relationships, then he might be in a stronger position to leave the company and get longer-term help with relationships.

Beatrice and Nigel meet over the next few months and Nigel proves to be a difficult client with whom to relate and work. He is often depressed and then gets into 'blaming-the-world-mode'. He is sometimes demanding (once appearing without an appointment and demanding to be seen), and shows little ability to understand anyone else's opinion. He is continually in 'victim stance' and continues to threaten publicity after leaving the company.

As discussed in supervision, Beatrice suggests a three-way meeting a month before Nigel is due to leave. Her hope is that this might provide a forum for Nigel to deal with this un-finished company business and that he might be able to leave and let go of the company. She facilitates a meeting between the CEO, Nigel and herself in which she encourages Nigel to share his thoughts and feelings. The meeting seems to go well. The CEO listens and understands and advises Nigel to move ahead in his life, leaving behind the past. Nothing is mentioned about the threats.

A few days after the meeting Nigel has a 'breakdown', goes to his GP and is admitted to a psychiatric hospital. Beatrice contacts the psychiatrist and they agree to work together so that Nigel can be helped medically and psychologically. Nigel leaves the hospital a week later and sees Beatrice one more time before telling her he is not returning for counselling. He takes his early retirement and soon after phones the CEO to tell him he is approaching the papers with his revelations.

Throughout supervision the main areas covered have been:

- how to help Nigel in the short term deal with immediate problems;
- how to help Nigel in the longer term deal with deeper issues;
- how to look after the organization and the threat to its good name;
- how to help Beatrice make decisions that keep the needs of the individual and the needs of the company in perspective;
- how to harness the various helpers (doctor, occupational health, psychiatrist and counsellor) so that they work in unison and not against one another.

This example is given, not to offer supervisory solutions, but to reveal some of the critical issues that arise within supervision when there is a workplace organization involved. They bring into sharp relief some of the 11 tasks outlined above.

Conclusion

Supervision is for the welfare of clients (BAC 1995). Indirectly it works with supervisees to enable them to work more effectively with clients. But neither clients nor counsellors exist in vacuums –

they both belong to systems that impact on their work together. In the case of the client these systems will include family and friends, communities and of course the workplace. For supervisees there will be similar influences from similar cultures. All of these contexts are valid focus-points for supervision since any or all can at any stage be influential in the counselling work. Because workplace counsellors work with employees who belong to the same organization as themselves it is imperative that supervisors bring to supervision knowledge of organizations, of counselling, of counselling management and ways in which counselling can be integrated with other roles and other organizational functions. This is not an easy task, but it is never dull.

References

BAC (British Association for Counselling) (1995) *Code of Ethics and Practice for Supervisors*. Rugby: British Association for Counselling.

Bernard, J. and Goodyear, R. (1992) *Fundamentals of Clinical Supervision*. Boston, MA: Allyn & Bacon.

Berridge, J., Cooper, C.L. and Highley-Marchington, C. (1997) *Employee Assistance Programmes and Workplace Counselling*. Chichester: Wiley.

Bull, A. (1997) 'Models of counselling in organizations', in M. Carroll and M. Walton (eds) *The Handbook of Counselling in Organizations*. London: Sage.

Carroll, C. (1997) 'Building bridges: a study of employee counsellors in the private sector', in M. Carroll and M. Walton (eds) *The Handbook of Counselling in Organizations*. London: Sage.

Carroll, M. (1995) 'The generic tasks of supervision'. Unpublished Ph.D. Dissertation, University of Surrey.

—— (1996a) *Counselling Supervision: Theory, Skills and Practice*. London: Cassell.

—— (1996b) *Workplace Counselling: A Systematic Approach to Employee Care*. London: Sage.

—— (1997a) 'Counselling in the workplace: luxury or necessity?' Keynote address for conference on 'Counselling in the Workplace', March, St George's Conference Unit. London.

—— (1997b) 'Counselling in organizations: an overview', in M. Carroll and M. Walton (eds) *The Handbook of Counselling in Organizations*. London: Sage.

—— (1997c) (Private Publication) Lecture given at the University of Utrecht, The Netherlands, April.

Critchley, B. and Casey, D. (1989) 'Organizations get stuck too'. *Leadership and Organization Development Journal*, 10 (4): 3–12.

Egan, G. (1994) *Working the Shadow-Side: A Guide to Positive Behind-the-Scenes Management*. San Francisco, CA: Jossey-Bass.

Hawkins, P. and Shohet, R. (1989) *Supervision in the Helping Professions*. Milton Keynes: Open University Press.

Holloway, E. (1995) *Clinical Supervision: A Systems Approach*. Thousand Oaks, CA: Sage.

Inskipp, F. and Proctor, B. (1993) *Making the Most of Supervision*, Part 1. Twickenham: Cascade Publications.

Inskipp, F. and Proctor, B. (1995) *Making the Most of Supervision*, Part 2. Twickenham: Cascade Publications.

Lane, D. (1990) 'Counselling psychology in organizations', *The Psychologist*, 12: 540–4.

Martin, I. (1996) *From Couch to Corporation: Becoming a Successful Corporate Therapist*. New York: Wiley.

Page, S. and Wosket, V. (1994) *Supervising the Counsellor: A Cyclical Model*. London: Routledge.

Proctor, B. (1997a) 'Contracts in supervision', in C. Sills (ed.) *Contracts in Counselling*. London: Sage.

Proctor, B. (1997b) 'Supervision for counsellors in organizations', in M. Carroll and M. Walton (eds) *The Handbook of Counselling in Organizations*. London: Sage.

Sperry, L. (1996) *Corporate Therapy and Consulting*. New York: Brunner/Mazel.

Walton, M. (1997a) 'Counselling as a form of organizational change', in M. Carroll and M. Walton (eds) *The Handbook of Counselling in Organizations*. London: Sage.

Walton, M. (1997b) 'Organizational culture and its impact on counselling', in M. Carroll and M. Walton (eds) *The Handbook of Counselling in Organizations*. London: Sage.

9 Supervision in religious settings

Elizabeth Mann

In the UK and the USA, the religious context for supervision is at present predominantly either the Anglican Communion, the Catholic Church, or the Nonconformist churches which have a wide range of denominations. In all of these, there is an underlying basis of the Christian religion. This chapter will focus upon supervision of counselling which is in some way related to these particular settings. However it is important to hold in mind the wider context of different religions. An increasingly multi-cultural society, increasing ease of mobility, and identification of supervision needs in workplaces engaged with other cultures, may bring counsellors into contact with a diversity of clients' religious backgrounds. This in turn is a challenge to the supervisor to be reflective about the contextual commonalities and differences between the religious backgrounds encountered by supervisees. It is hoped that the specifics of this chapter may stimulate the reader to reflect upon the generalities of this wider religious context, and to draw relevance from the issues presented to derive a more comprehensive sensitivity.

This chapter will highlight specific issues of counsellors and clients in religious settings in the generic tasks of supervision, that is, relationship, teaching, counselling, ethical monitoring, evaluation, consultation and administration (Carroll 1996). It will also address supervision issues at the interface with the religious organization within which the counselling takes place.

The counsellors

Where there is a religious context for the client, the counsellor may fall into one of three categories. First, there are those who are themselves priests, ministers or Religious. ('Religious' is used here as the formal nomenclature of those who live under vows in religious communities which have a structured lifestyle based on contemplation or specialized ministry or both.) Second, there are counsellors who are lay members of churches, where their personal values may to some extent be rooted. Third, there are counsellors who do not identify themselves with the religious/church context and values, but who work with clients who do.

There are particularly important supervision issues for counsellors in a religious setting who are themselves priests or ministers, issues which may be summarized in psychodynamic terms as countertransference issues. The supervisor, as the guardian of the ethics of the counselling engagement, has a professional responsibility to help counsellors continually to check out to what extent their own issues are driving interventions and interpretations, collusions and avoidance, in the counselling sessions.

There is some evidence that a shared religious belief system between counsellor and client may act as a resistance in therapy (Kehoe and Gutheil 1984). One significant issue may be a shared loyalty to the image of the church, which both Religious and priest-clients and counsellors may collude to preserve as good, since the church is the place where their identity is rooted, particularly for those in religious life. In practice, this collusion may result in a mutual avoidance in therapy of issues which are seen to be damaging to the image.

Monica's priest-supervisee was counselling a priest-client who suffered disabling guilt feelings after committing a criminal offence, which he had kept secret. She found her supervisee very reluctant to address the secrecy issue in the counselling, for fear of the effect on the image of the church if the client then disclosed his offence.

For priest-counsellors, the church is also the ultimate source of their livelihood. Miller and Atkinson (1988) claim an unethical conflict of interest obtains between the clergyman in role as minister and in role as counsellor to the group on which he or she depends for material benefit. Such a conflict may be experienced by any other workplace counsellor, but supervisors of counsellors in a religious setting need to be aware of the specific contextual issues. In practice in the church, there may be uncertainty about the nature of the relationships and the consequent boundaries between pastoral care, spiritual direction, the use of counselling skills in ministerial roles, and professional counselling *per se*, and the stipendiary implications of these roles and responsibilities. Krebs (1980) cited in Miller and Atkinson (1988) concluded that for the clergyperson as counsellor, there were irresolvable problems of transference, role confusion misplaced pastoral priorities and lay expectations of cheap therapy. Miller and Atkinson analysed these four areas, and discerned a common theme of a conflict between the expectations of the client and their feelings about the divine on the one hand, and the professional commitment of the clergyperson as counsellor on the other. They confirm that in ministry it is very difficult to prevent the dual relationships which could impair counsellors' professional judgement and contravene their professional code of ethics. They argue that dilemmas arising from transference and countertransference might quickly subvert the possibility of a therapeutic relationship. On the other hand, McLeod (1993) has argued that humanistic approaches to counselling might allow more boundary flexibility than analytic or dynamic orientations. C. Carroll's research (1994) found that employee counsellors see themselves enjoying a wide variety of roles. Whichever view is held by the supervisee, it is part of the ethical task of supervision to monitor and evaluate multiplicity of roles and implications of stipends.

In the case of chaplains, roles and responsibilities may be written into the employment contract, or the supervisor may be able to facilitate clarification in supervision or in tripartite meetings with administrators from the employing organization.

One of Monica's supervisees, Sheila, was a university chaplain, who was a trained counsellor. In an analysis of her work in supervision, some confusion of expectations about her roles and responsibilities was identified. Following on supervision consultation, Sheila was able to negotiate with the university authorities a clarification of how these different roles might be contained within her employment duties, and how her counselling might be distinctively contracted, bounded, resourced, financed and supervised.

Bob was a stipendiary Anglican clergyman who had had some counselling training and wanted to offer counselling to the members of his church congregation. He consulted Monica because he found a role conflict was arising when he was trying to build up a therapeutic relationship in counselling with a parishioner and at the same time coming into conflict with the person in the business of the church council. In supervision with Monica, Bob clarified that he could not ethically sustain both relationships simultaneously, and that his employment as a parish priest precluded working as a professional counsellor with his own parishioners. Bob found himself in a very painful dilemma. On the principle that major personal issues arising in supervision should be taken to personal therapy (Lesser 1984), Monica referred Bob to facilitate him to make his choice between them. Bob eventually opted to train further as a professional therapist and left his parish to work full-time for a counselling agency.

Supervisors working with counsellors who had first trained and been ordained as priests have found a high incidence of counter-transference issues concerned with sexuality. Both priest-clients and priest-counsellors may have unresolved issues because of confusion about their orientation, uncertainty about their commitment to celibacy, or naivety in sexual relationships. Supervisors need to be aware that priests and Religious who began training at an early age may have had little or no formal education in sexual development, and that the ethos of their formation and community life may have precluded open discussion of sexual relationships.

James was a priest who presented with problems of resentment about lack of promotion by his bishop. He engaged in therapy with Matthew, a priest-counsellor. Matthew's supervisor observed how much Matthew looked forward to his sessions with James and the extent of his sympathy for James which emerged in the sessions reported in supervision. Matthew, however, denied any emotional involvement with James. In the therapy, without reference to his supervisor, Matthew allowed himself to be manipulated into agreeing to approach James' bishop on James' behalf, to ask for some preferential treatment. When James was referred to another counsellor who was not a priest, it transpired that James had a history of soliciting favours by means of sexual advances to other men. Matthew had naively allowed himself to be manipulated in this way without any intra-personal emotional awareness of what was happening.

In this case, James told the lay counsellor that he would never have disclosed his history to another priest. Research offers some confirming evidence that a client may be evasive in therapy with a priest-counsellor. Francis (1979) found a significant difference in the direction of increased score falsification when a religious attitude test was administered by a priest rather than a lay person.

Peter, a priest-counsellor, brought a tape to supervision of an early session with a priest-client who had been referred on his admission of activities of child sex abuse. The tape revealed an almost complete lack of response on the part of the counsellor in the session. When Peter's supervisor explored this, it transpired that the client and the counsellor had been ordained at the same place on the same occasion, and this disclosure had evoked such strong emotions in the counsellor, who had some unresolved issues about his own vocation and sexuality, that he was unable to engage with the client. He had been unaware of the effect on the counselling of this.

For some priest supervisees, therefore, countertransference issues with religious clients may be strongly present, and the monitoring of these, and the allied parallel processes, will be particularly important in the supervision relationship and consultancy tasks. In contrast, priest-counsellors who have worked through these issues for themselves in personal therapy will have the particular strength of their experiential understanding, which will empower them in working with clients who have the same problems.

To some extent counsellors who are lay members of churches have a similar advantage in that they have some experiential understanding of a priest-client's religious context, cognitions and values. The relevance and importance of this contextual under-standing seems to be borne out by research. Wallace (1985) found that issues brought to therapy by priests and Religious clients are no different from those of psychotherapy patients in general; however, because of the unique lifestyle of the priest and Religious client, the manifestations and the resolutions of the issues may differ. It seems to follow, therefore, that the contextual under-standing is necessary for both effective diagnosis and effective intervention, and therefore it may form a significant part of the teaching or information-giving tasks of supervision with lay supervisees.

Additionally, it has been observed in counselling practice that priests may gain insight from a counsellor's use of analogies, as that is a learning methodology which seems to transfer particularly well from their discipline of theology. It seems, therefore, that the use of analogies which are grounded in the particular religious context and its values, could effectively be employed in the teaching task of supervision, and could then be reflected and used in the client's learning process within the therapy. The lay super-visee who is well informed of the religious context, but at the same time is less affected by the transference and countertransference issues, seems to be in a particularly advantageous position for working with priests and Religious clients in this way.

Supervisees who do not identify with a religious context themselves, but who work with clients who do, have the strength of a greater objectivity, but usually need to become more informed. There is to some extent a debate about how much the lay counsellor needs to know the religious context of the client. Clearly such knowledge is facilitating, though as we have already begun to see, too much involvement of the counsellor in a specific context without self-awareness may be damaging to the client, and this will be the supervisor's professional responsibility to discern and address with the counsellor. On the other hand, insufficient knowledge of the religious context will be a limitation in counselling diagnosis and methodology. In such cases, modelling the use of the religious context will be one of the relevant teaching tasks of supervision.

It is particularly important for those counsellors who do not identify with the values of the religious context to explore their own values in supervision, and the extent to which these values influence the interventions with their clients (Corey 1996). The supervisor has the ethical responsibility to clarify whose needs are being met, the client's or the counsellor's, in the value judgements inherent in the counselling interventions. Counsellors cannot be value-free. However, an essential element of the task of monitoring professional/ethical issues in supervision will be monitoring the supervisee's facilitation of the client to achieve his or her goals within the framework of the client's own religious value systems.

The clients

The religious contexts of clients may vary from a community life formally structured under lifetime vows of obedience and celibacy, to a priesthood lived and practised in a parish or gathered congregational setting less separated from society. The religious commitment may be rooted in upbringing in the family, or may be a commitment of personal choice. It is important for the supervisor to be able to differentiate between such groups, because the underlying client issues may be very different.

First, there are clients who are Religious themselves. Typically, they have left their families and 'entered' their religious communities, sometimes at quite a young age, where they pursue a long academic and spiritual formation (that is, training for ordination in the case of a priest) in the context of a separated, celibate, community lifestyle. The second group of clients are Catholic 'secular' or diocesan priests, Anglican clergy and Nonconformist ministers, who are increasingly able to enter training for ministry at any age, and may have some considerable prior experience in employment or professional practice, and whose choice for ministry may have been made at a more mature age. These clients may lead lives less sequestered from society than their religious counterparts, and their identity may be less foreclosed. They may be in more healthy stages of identity moratorium or maturity. The third group of clients are lay clients who have varying degrees of attachment to their churches and religious groups, and varying commitments to particular religious beliefs, values and practices which originate from their current religious group or from their family background. They may be spouses or children of clergy, in which case supervision may provide an opportunity for a systemic analysis if that has not been done already.

The training/formation process for priests has traditionally placed a high value on rational thought, but in the past the curriculum has not included human and sexual development, nor encouraged reflection on experience, emotional awareness or the ability to manage feelings. Priest-clients may often present, therefore, with a highly intellectual approach to their problems, and at the same time show an unexpected naivety about emotional and sexual matters. Keddy, Erdberg and Sammon (1990), in a study of male and female Catholic clergy and Religious referred for treatment, found that the clients exhibited an intellectualized orientation, naive defensiveness and difficulty in handling emotions. Twenty-eight per cent were confused or distressed about their sexual orientation.

The predominant underlying issues in the counselling of Religious and celibate priests seem to be issues of identity, sexuality and intimacy: identity with respect to issues of choice and commitment, and expectations of a persona of priesthood which militate against the search for a personal identity; sexuality with respect to guilt about masturbation, confusion about orientation and problems of inappropriate acting out; intimacy with respect to loneliness in community life, combined with low self-esteem and low self-acceptance. These issues are, of course, not discrete but interdependent.

Identity: choice and commitment

Religious priests and Brothers who are now in middle age or older often left their families for the religious life at a young, pre-adolescent age. At the mid-life stage, a review of achievement seems to be generally quite normal (Levinson 1978). What seems to be particular at this stage of life to many priests and Religious who have come for counselling, however, is an upsurge of doubt about their commitment. It is often rooted in a foreclosed identity, where the foreclosure has been made under the influence of parents in pre-teen years, or religious, parental or hero figures in teenage years. When the priest reaches mid-life, he finds it difficult to change to the identity moratorium he needs in order to progess towards finding his own mature identity.

Luke is a middle-aged priest who became aware of these issues of choice and commitment in therapy. He said 'I realize now that I have never made a free choice in my life. It's very frightening.'

There is an underlying issue here which is well illustrated by the classic theory of Erikson (1981). In Erikson's terms, when pre-adolescents have made a commitment to the church before they have explored their own identity, the stage of identity formation has been missed out. This has prejudiced the smooth development of the subsequent stage of intimacy and perhaps a later potential for generativity. Instead, the middle-aged priest gets stuck in role-confusion and isolation, which can lead to depression and apathy.

Martin is a priest-client in his mid-forties who was drawn into the church as a lonely child and responded to encouragement to a vocation to the priesthood from an age of 11 years. In therapy, he recognized that he had never experienced a normal adolescence, and the sight of teenagers enjoying themselves in the street caused him strong feelings of sadness and envy. Part of the counselling experience for Martin was grieving for his lost adolescence, and part of Monica's task as supervisor was to ensure that the counsellor facilitated Martin to work through that grief, rather than avoid it under the pressure of the other issues which Martin brought simultaneously to the counselling, and then to plan how the counsellor might help Martin begin exploring his identity for the first time.

Priests who are currently in their twenties or early thirties may have entered religious life during their teenage years, and may have experienced this syndrome. Some, a minority, will have entered later, after some experience of training or employment outside the parameters of religious life. These men are more likely to have a mature identity and are more able to use therapy for their personal development with less struggle. The supervisor needs to facilitate the supervisee to explore with the client the influences and dynamics preceding the transitions into religious life or the commitment to the ordination process, and assess the degree of choice underlying the commitment which has been made.

Priest-counsellors who have worked through this process themselves will inevitably have a sharp awareness of these issues and an attendant capacity for empathy with the client. Supervisees with no religious contextual background may be less sensitive to this identity issue, and it may need to be one of the teaching tasks of supervision.

All priests and ministers are under the external pressures of expectations of a persona of priesthood which militates against the search for and growth towards personal identity. Some clients may be resistant to facing the challenge of exploring their own identity and the changes this growth process may demand.

Joe, a middle-aged priest, said in counselling 'I am under so many expectations, I don't know who I am any more.' Marion, his counsellor, felt helpless in the face of this statement. In supervision, Monica and Marion worked to differentiate the roles inherent in Joe's priesthood and personal life as a means of challenging him to seek his identity.

Sexuality

Catholic secular priests, as well as the Religious, are under a vow of celibacy. There is also a minority of Anglican priests who make a commitment to celibacy by choice, although they are not required to do so by their church. These clients may have sexual issues related to celibacy underlying their presenting problems, and the consultancy task of supervision may therefore involve exploration of these and the associated countertransference issues.

The substantive issue for the supervisor is to have knowledge about these sexual issues and the processes which might emerge in relation to them in supervision. Priest-supervisees may have particular countertransference issues which need to be addressed in their own personal therapy. Lay supervisees may have latent judgemental or intolerant attitudes of which they need to become self-aware in supervision, and likewise perhaps to take to their own therapy.

In recent years, a growing number of cases of sexual abuse by priests has come to light. The offenders have often been highly intellectual men, apparently sincerely committed to their ministry. They express bewilderment at what has happened and that no one seems to be able to understand them or help them. Character-istically, they are unaware that they are committing a criminal offence, and they find it extremely difficult to understand and to accept responsibility for the effect on the victim. This is in fact true of all sex offenders, not only priests. The difference which has been observed in the priest sex offender population is 'the woeful ignorance . . . an almost pathetic lack of knowledge and sophistica-tion about all matters sexual among clergy and Religious' (Loftus and Camargo 1993: 300).

Walter was a leader in a boys' youth organization in a socially deprived inner city area. He was lonely and persuaded himself that to masturbate with young boys was a way of giving them the affection they needed. He justified to himself the morality of this by means of complex theologial and ethical arguments. When he admitted to his bishop that he had had physical sex with several juveniles, he was sent for therapy on a sex offender programme. Walter found it an intensely painful experience to be confronted with the fact that his relationship with the boys was not giving them affection as he had persuaded himself, but that he had been abusing them to meet his own needs.

The church hierarchy has tended to be protective of sexually abusing priests, out of respect for the office of priesthood and concern about the bad publicity for the church generated by cases of abuse. A conflict may arise between the desire of the church authorities to prevent disclosure of offences, and the therapeutic process for the client of moving from secrecy to openness. This may be compounded by a naivety which minimizes the serious-ness and criminal nature of the offences.

Edward came for a psychological assessment as a normal part of his training programme. It was found that he was a high risk for sexually abusing boys of a certain age in the youth club which he ran. He spoke openly about his sexual fantasies but was quite naive as to how close he was to acting them out. The church authorities responsible for the youth club were resistant to making a change of appointment, preferring the risk of an offence to the risk of disclosure of the problem.

The church hierarchy has additionally tended to be protective of sexually abusing priests because of a sensitivity to the magnitude of the loss for a priest if his offence becomes public. The counsellor may become very sympathetic to the priest-client in the same way, and be reluctant to make a referral which would result in a disclosure of the offence. In such situations, a supervisor has professional responsibility to clarify unequivocally that it would be unethical for the supervisee to attempt to treat the client themselves. Supervisors need to know what professional treatment programmes are available, and to insist on referrals, however great the loss of the client to the counsellor, the cost in time and fees to the church organization, and however much patient explanation is needed to be given to the church authorities to effect this. In this respect, the supervisor may have to be, even if indirectly, the ethical conscience for the church.

Clients who are Anglican priests or Nonconformist ministers, are free to marry, and generally to have a lifestyle similar to those who are not formally in ministry. This does not necessarily preclude the kinds of problems described above, but other problems may present in counselling such as stress and breakdown in priests' and ministers' marriage relationships. Clergy often experience a high degree of ambiguity at the boundary between family/home and work spheres (Lee 1995), but in the consultancy task of supervision, an exploration may show that this masks deeper relationship and sexual problems.

Julie's presenting problem was the feeling that she could no longer go on in her marriage. She said to her counsellor that her priest husband was so obsessive in 'serving' the parish that he had no time for her or for the children. Days off and holidays were invaded by parish business and the marriage relationship seemed dead. Julie's husband refused to go to counselling. Supervision gave Julie's counsellor the opportunity to explore the resistances, underlying which there proved to be sexual problems on both sides. In the therapy Julie gained so much insight into this that she was able to resolve her own sexual problem and help her husband with his. She taught him how to enjoy sex, and the practicalities of the boundary problem were resolved as an outcome.

Intimacy

The obverse of intimacy is loneliness. Counselling practice and recent research have revealed a marked incidence of loneliness in clients from religious communities. A priest's loyalty to his community militates against the disclosure of his painful and angry feelings. Yet strong tensions are played out in relationship problems, often between those whose identities have been formed within the traditional rule-based ethos, and the younger, more flexibly minded priests. Priests may feel bewildered, disturbed and alone in the midst of these relationship tensions and conflicts. In the community, grief may be unrecognized and unresolved, skills of intimacy and conflict resolution may be unknown and there may often be patterns of withdrawal into isolation.

Stephen is a Religious priest who is also a gifted musician. He was referred to therapy because of his increasing withdrawal from life in the community. On one occasion he withdrew to his room for three days after a momentary criticism from a confrère about a piece of litter he had dropped in a common room. When his presenting problem was brought to supervision, it proved that as well as underlying issues of shame, he had no intimacy or conflict-resolution skills with which to manage his loneliness.

Supervisors need to be aware of the correlation between loneliness and low self-esteem in religious clients. From his research, Sullivan (1987) concluded that the self-images of the Religious were typically distorted. They tended to see themselves as less adequate and more inferior than others saw them. They compared their self-image against the ideal they had developed for themselves in their religious life, and felt badly about themselves. Moulds and McCabe (1991) concluded that the need for approval remains a fundamental construct among Religious.

The organization

In every counselling or supervision session where there is a religious context, there is present, either overtly or covertly, recognized or unrecognized, acknowledged or unacknowledged, the religious organization.

For the majority of priests and ministers, this will be the diocese or Nonconformist regional area, headed by a bishop or chairman, with a delegated management structure which has traditionally been hierarchical and authoritarian. The same kind of structure occurs on a smaller scale in religious orders and communities, where the Superior General or local Superior heads a council to whom the vow of obedience applies. Older priests and ministers will have been trained under this authoritarian structure. Younger ones will be experiencing a change of ethos generated by the Second Vatican Council in the Catholic Church, or by the evolution of more consultative management styles in society which are gradually taken on board by church hierarchies.

In the Catholic Church, the massive prescription of change from the Second Vatican Council for the church in general, and for religious communities in particular, has led to a transition which has been, and still is, very stressful to implement. This transition is essentially from an authoritarian, highly structured lifestyle to an ethos of mutual consultation, flexible individualized training and management by consensus.

A sociological case study of the community transition as it was experienced by the Passionist religious order describes the long period of painful struggle in the community dynamics, enduring for decades rather than years (Sweeney 1994).

The supervisor also needs to know that there have been in the past identity issues of churches which have made access to counselling difficult for priests, ministers and Religious. A theological identity has been held as distinct from, and even incompatible with, a psychological form of thought. This has been partly due to the traditional churches' fears that psychology might be in conflict with theology, and, in particular, that psychology might be destructive, and 'explain away' faith. This in turn may have led to denial of priests' problems, or avoidance of openness to psychological assessment and help. Church hierarchies have at times been reluctant to back psychological research. Arbuckle (1988) claims that social scientists have been marginalized within the church, because of denial of reality, for example of crises which are disturbing to the church hierarchy, or because of attempts to cope with chaos by withdrawal into an unreal spiritual world.

Figure 9.1   *The quadruple supervisory relationship*

However, the present climate is more favourable to growing collaboration. The supervisor needs to be aware of the particular ethos in which the counsellor is working in this respect.

Supervision in a religious context is necessarily supervision in an organizational context, and the relevant theory (Carroll 1996) needs to be known and applied. Within the religious context there will not generally be a simple linear model of supervisor to counsellor to client, unless the arrangements have been made independently. Where the organization is the context, the model will be a quadruple relationship which, directly or indirectly, will connect the client, the counsellor, the organization and the supervisor (Figure 9.1).

The task of the supervisor is to comprehend the internal dynamics of this quadruple relationship and be able to interpret them at any given moment to the counsellor. This will necessitate an understanding of the structure and culture of the organization – whether the religious community, the diocese or other administrative region – and the dynamics of its management council.

Up to the time of writing, there has been no model for the supervision of counselling of priests which is based both on their particular contextual and identity issues and also on the organizational issues of their vocations in the structures and culture of the church. The supervisor needs to be able to think systemically as well as intrapersonally, when her supervisee has a client from a religious community. A systemic map of a community is a useful aid in a supervision session. A *sine qua non* of the reflexivity in the consultancy task of supervision will be processing the dynamics of the organization, not least the 'shadow-side' of these (Egan 1994). Egan, who is himself a priest, discusses the anatomy of organizational politics and relates those to the issues of competition, self-interest, power and political strategy. A supervisee who is developing an effective counselling service within an organization cannot afford to be unaware of these issues. Yates (1985), posits that 'when government agencies, businesses, churches and educational institutions are ranked for the virulence of their politics, churches tend to be easy winners' (cited in Egan 1994: 195). It follows that the supervisor of a counsellor who is working in a religious organization needs to be able to reflect systemically with the supervisee in this shadow-side dimension.

Case study

June was asked by a bishop to set up a professional counselling service which would offer assessment and therapy to priests, ordinands and other ministers in the diocese. (The diocese is the largely independent regional unit of management and administration in the Anglican and Catholic churches). June looked for a consultant supervisor who would understand the religious context of the clients and who also had a wide theoretical knowledge and practical experience of counselling in organizations. She made an independent consultant supervision contract with Paul, who suggested meeting regularly once each month but with flexibility of availabilty if there were immediate organizational issues arising at the counsellor–diocese interface. June explained this arrangement to the bishop who accepted it without reservation, without desiring to be personally involved. He was content to trust June to consult where necessary and report back to him any outcomes of the supervision which would contribute to the development and smooth operation of the service.

From meetings with key management personnel in the diocese, June elicited the client and organizational issues which needed to be resolved. In supervision with Paul, these issues were analysed both separately and at the client–diocese interface. In subsequent supervision sessions, the developmental needs of the new service were analysed. The philosophy of the service, its aims and goals, the differentiation from other diocesan pastoral care systems, the governance of the scheme, the financial implications, the relevant ethical and professional issues, and the dissemination strategy were explored, rehearsed, refined and shaped into policies. Then June role-played her approaches to the diocesan management with these policies. She also role-played the responses of the diocesan management in a search to understand their reactions and problems.

June's attention to the client–organization interface took up a much greater proportion of her time than she had expected. She discovered the need to listen at length to people in the diocesan management structure with key roles who would be directly or tangentially linked to the operation of the new counselling scheme. She came to understand that the impact of the religious organization on the client was a fundamental issue in assessment in the counselling process. The counselling process in turn provided valuable feedback for both the development of the counselling service and, more widely, the healthy development of the religious organization itself. Supervision time was used to map the management structure, to analyse its dynamics systemically, to discuss and refine draft reports and reflect upon policy development. None of this would have been possible without Paul's knowledge and experience of organizational management as well as of counselling psychology. June noticed and appreciated at the same time that Paul maintained a balance on the supervision agenda and in supervision time so that individual client work was never sacrificed disproportionately under the demands of the organizational challenges. In practice, Paul's supervision of June's work not only helped her to develop and manage the new counselling service, but also to maintain high ethical and professional standards of client work.

One of the most demanding challenges in practice pertaining to the religious context was an ethical resolution of confidentiality issues. The referrals were usually made and the costs of the counselling borne by the diocese. Consequently, the bishop and his staff, or the diocesan training officer, expected some feedback from the counselling process when a client had a psychological problem or a personal development need during training for ordination. June needed to work with the diocese to develop a tailor-made three-way confidentiality agreement for the release of relevant information to the bishop or his nominated representative in these circumstances. This was a new experience in the church, where in the past such issues had been resolved either by an expectation of good will or by traditional values of obedience. However, June was aware that this traditional model was inadequate both as a professional protection of the client and a protection against litigation for the bishop. As she developed a pro-forma for the three-way confidentiality agreement, she needed to have this monitored by an ethically competent supervisor. So she negotiated back and forth with the diocese to develop a series of drafts which she brought to her sessions with Paul for evaluation, with the result that a pro-forma was finally produced which was acceptable to clients and diocese and was also legally adequate.

Not least, supervision for June was a place where she could bring her questions and feelings about the organization. Sometimes development went fast and well. At other times there were frustrating delays due to organizational bureaucracy, or to fear of what to the church were new ideas or procedures. Supervision enabled June to adjust her perspectives and strategies when she experienced negative feelings which might otherwise have inhibited her work. Additionally, supervision proved to be a place where June could feel confident that she would be monitored in looking after herself professionally in a way she could not necessarily expect from the church organization she was serving.

Summary

Supervision in a religious setting has its own particular contextual issues arising from the structure and culture of the religious organization. It seems to be a necessity in effective counselling that the supervisor should know the religious context well, and ensure through supervision that supervisees acquire and continually enhance this knowledge and reflect upon its implications for their interpretations and interventions. Important areas for religious clients are those of identity, sexuality and intimacy. Perhaps the most significant hazard to obviate is that of unrecognized countertransference.

Similarly, an exploration and analysis of the organization will be an inherent challenge in the supervision process. If the supervisor does not know the organizational structure, and is not able to promote reflexivity on the organizational dynamics, the result might be a misunderstanding of the work of the counsellor within the organization. If the supervisor is not able to promote the supervisee's reflexivity on the effect of the organization upon the client, there may be a lack of effectiveness in evoking change.

A knowledge of, and working relationship with, the religious organization, will be essential in facilitating and monitoring the supervisee's confidentiality procedures, and in issues of client resistance to psychological help.

It is not necessary for supervisors or supervisees to have religious beliefs and values which are identical with those of the clients in the setting of the counselling. However, it seems to be essential for effective outcomes that they should know the context very well. Particularly in the relationship, consultative and ethical monitoring tasks of supervision, contextual knowledge and insight will be a *sine qua non* of supervisee facilitation and client change.

References

Arbuckle, G.A. (1988) 'The marginalisation of social scientists within the church', *Human Development*, 10 (2): 16–21.

Carroll, C. (1994) 'Building bridges: a study of employee counsellors in the private sector', MSc dissertation, City University, London.

Carroll, M. (1996) *Counselling Supervision: Theory, Skills and Practice*, London: Cassell.

Corey, G. (1996) *Theories and Practice in Counselling and Psychotherapy*, 5th edn. Pacific Grove, CA: Brookes/Cole.

Egan, G. (1994) *Working the Shadow-Side: A Guide to Positive Behind-the-Scenes Management*, San Francisco, CA: Jossey-Bass.

Erikson, E.H. (1981) *Identity and the Life Cycle*, New York: Norton.

Francis, L.J. (1979) 'The priest as administrator in attitude research', *Journal for the Scientific Study of Religion*, 18 (1): 78–81.

Keddy, P.J., Erdberg, P. and Sammon, S.D. (1990) 'The psychological assessment of Catholic clergy and religious referred for residential treatment', *Pastoral Psychology*, 38 (3): 147–59.

Kehoe, N. and Gutheil, T.G. (1984) 'Shared religious belief as resistance in psychotherapy', *American Journal of Psychotherapy*, 38 (4): 579–85.

Krebs, R. (1980) 'Why Pastors should not be Counsellors', *The Journal of Pastoral Care*, 34 (4): 229–33.

Lee, C. (1995) 'Rethinking boundary ambiguity from an ecological perspective: stress in Protestant clergy families', *Family Process*, 34 (1): 75–86.

Lesser, R.M. (1984) 'Supervision: illusions, anxieties and questions', in L. Caligor, P.M. Bromberg and J.D. Meltzer (eds) *Clinical Perspectives on the Supervision of Psychoanalysis and Psychotherapy*. New York: Plenum Press.

Levinson, D.J. (1978) *The Seasons of a Man's Life*. New York: Ballantine.

Loftus, S.J. and Camargo, R.J. (1993) 'Treating the clergy', *Annals of Sex Research*, 6: 287–308.

McLeod, J. (1993) *The Organizational Context of Counselling*, Centre for Counselling Studies: Keele University.

Miller, H.M.L. and Atkinson, D.R. (1988) 'The clergyperson as counsellor: an inherent conflict of interest', *Counselling and Values*, 32 (2) (January): 116–23.

Moulds, J.D. and McCabe, M.P. (1991) 'Self-acceptance in a Catholic male religious congregation', *Australian Psychologist*, 26 (3): 197–202.

Sullivan, J.E. (1987) *Journey to Freedom: the Path to Self-Esteem for the Priesthood and Religious Life*, New York: Paulist Press.

Sweeney, J. (1994) *The New Religious Order*, London: Belliew.

Wallace, A.M. (1985) 'Initial encounters of religious and priests with psychotherapy', *Psychotherapy Patient*, 1 (3): 147–58.

Yates, D., Jr (1985) *The Politics of Management: Exploring the Inner Workings of Public and Private Organizations*. San Fransisco, CA: Jossey-Bass.

10 Supervision in uniformed settings

John Towler

Supervising counsellors who work in organizations can be a mixture of intense excitement and challenge, holding ambiguity, tensions, and 'not-knowing', all in the space where supervisee, client and organization are to be honoured. We could learn well from following the motto of the Constructive Therapists (de Shazer 1985):

What works, do more of it.
If it's not working, do something different.
If it works, don't fix it.

The theme of this chapter is how counsellors and supervisors alike manage the impact of organizational culture on supervision. Supervisors spend a considerable amount of time and energy helping supervisees field the impact of organizational culture. In this respect supervision might well be described as a 'counter-cultural' activity.

The chapter is written from the experience of an external supervisor working in both one-to-one and group formats with an internal counselling service of one UK Police Service. It is offered as a contribution to the debate highlighted by Holloway (1995: 98) that 'the influence of organization variables on supervision has

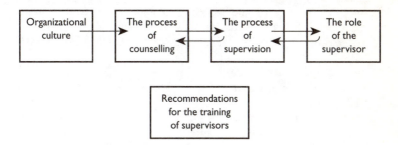

Figure 10.1 *The counter-cultural flow*

rarely been studied'. The shape of the chapter can best be expressed diagrammatically (Figure 10.1).

Organizational culture

Morgan (1986: 128) provides a well-accepted definition of culture as:

> shared meaning, shared understanding, and shared sense making . . . a process of reality construction allows people to see and understand particular events, actions, objects, utterances, or situations in distinctive ways.

Many writers have attempted to classify types of organizational culture (Hawkins and Shohet 1989; Randall et al. 1980; Kets de Vries and Miller 1984; Harrison 1972; Handy 1993; Hawkins 1997). While avoiding the pitfalls of making types absolutist, each provides insight into particular emphases of organizational behaviour, values and beliefs. It is posited that police culture, while not neatly fitting any type, can be described as bureaucratic, power-based, paranoid, achievement-orientated, creating dependency.

The Sheehey Report (HMSO 1993) identifies four objectives for policing – preventing crime; bringing law-breakers to justice; keeping the Queen's peace; and protecting, helping and reassuring the community.

While some of the following cultural characteristics of the Police Service have research backing, others are offered from the experience of the writer:

- constant alertness and availability for public duty and maximum flexibility of response to diverse and rapidly changing priorities (Towler 1996);
- keeping strong for the public and each other in the maintenance of law and order, safety and in crisis (Towler 1996);
- according to a cult of masculinity (Brown and Campbell 1994);
- a crisis and trauma-orientated business (Towler 1996);
- social isolation of organizational members (Brown and Campbell 1994);
- peer solidarity and resistance to self- and outside scrutiny and change (Brown and Campbell 1994);
- past reliance on informal practices (Brown and Campbell 1994);

- accelerated change to professionalized and specialized services, with the competing interests of paternalism versus achievement (Towler 1996);
- wrestling with the impact and application of equal opportunities policies;
- the power of the uniform and the hierarchy which is derived from rank;
- engagement with the struggle of good versus evil.

The context and role of counsellors

Organizational counsellors are expected to juggle with a multiplicity of roles (Towler 1997). Roles for welfare counsellors include 'pastor', debt counsellor, befriender and supporter, crisis counsellor, psychological debriefer, stress manager, supervisor, report writer, on-call worker, peer supporter, team member, chair of meetings, and promoter of the service. They work alongside other professionals such as doctors, psychiatrists, occupational health personnel; and are rostered for a 24-hour on-call duty. Acting as purveyors and validators of their own services, counsellors:

- make presentations of their services;
- make detailed monthly statistical returns;
- submit their work to a research element through occasional papers, for example impact of sickness absence;
- share in the development of organizational protocols and standards;
- have a high-profile role in managing, developing and delivering trauma-support programmes.

Many of these activities create useful if heated debates as 'the culture of counselling' meets 'the culture of the organization'.

Supervision and culture

Before exploring the impact of culture on supervision, the following indicates the focus-points of supervision from the supervisor's perspective:

- being 'here' and 'there' for supervisee and organization
- the therapeutic/working alliance

- supervisee development
- tasks and functions of supervision
- influence of organizational context and culture
- strategies and techniques
- managing the supervisory relationship from assessment to ending
- skill interventions
- case conceptualization
- ethical dimensions
- levels of communication – verbal and non-verbal.

One of the chief tasks of the supervisor is developing and maintaining open communication with supervisees and service managers. Regular business meetings with managers provide opportunities for information sharing, dealing with issues such as boundary overlap, and building a strong working relationship.

The phenomenon of 'parallel process' in supervision

'Parallel process' is a fractal phenomenon (Gleick 1988) in which aspects of the counselling process are re-enacted or mirrored in the supervisory process. Supervisors need to be alert to the impact of this phenomenon on both the counselling and supervisory processes in the organizational context (Carroll 1996b; Clarkson 1995; Crandell and Allen 1982). Examples will be highlighted in the course of the chapter.

Impact of cultural characteristics on counselling and supervision

CONSTANT ALERTNESS, AVAILABILITY AND FLEXIBILITY   The unsociable hours worked by police officers are mirrored in the experience of counsellors who speak of lost sleep, restriction on social activity, and the need to be constantly alert as they experience the pressure of being 'on call' at night and at weekends. Checking the emotional and physical safety of counsellors in supervision is essential, that is, starting supervision sessions with a check as to the well-being of supervisees.

Some of the issues faced by counsellors are clients failing to turn up without notice, changing appointments at the last minute or requesting appointments outside hours. Coupled with the considerable demands of the role and domestic/social obligations, counsellors frequently feel pressurized, which results in frustration, anger, and in missed supervision sessions through unconscious or conscious attention elsewhere. Often the supervisor feels squeezed for time, pressurized by counsellors for solutions, or interrupted by requests by managers to 'pop into my office for a moment'.

Thus, managing and containing time boundaries, working with 'what is possible' and agreeing what cannot be worked with in the session, is paramount. At times, the supervisor is still fielding demands while leaving the building! Creating a safe, trusting relationship and 'practising' a quality of being with and for supervisees are part of the counter-cultural flow. This is but one example of 'parallel process' at work.

While the organization values physically and psychologically 'fit' counsellors, and recognizes the centrality of peer support, it also values the 'extra mile' without providing the resources – a confusion often expressed by supervisees. Managing the exasperation of supervisees, and holding multiple accountabilities, result in a constant tension for the supervisor.

The particular contracts in working with the UK Police Service are:

- Police Counselling Service with the external provider of supervision services;
- external supervisor with both the above, and with individual counsellors of the Police Counselling Service;
- individual supervisees with external supervisor and their Police Service clients.

Such accountabilities can best be expressed diagrammatically in the model of the 'three-cornered contract' (English 1975; Hay 1992; Towler 1997; Carroll 1996b) (Figure 10.2).

Hawkins and Shohet's (1989) definition of culture, distinguishes between organizational 'high-profile symbols' (the way it describes its services), and 'low-profile symbols' (the way it treats its staff). In this context, there is a lack of congruence between what protocol about supervision dictates (high-profile symbol) that is, the importance of regular weekly supervision, and what actually happens (low-profile symbol), for example where counsellors are seduced into more pressing activities such as meetings and trainings.

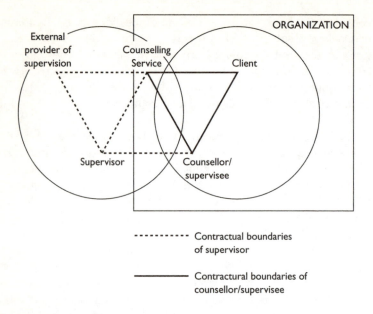

Figure 10.2   *The 'three-cornered contract': external provider of supervision for the Police Counselling Service*

Keeping strong, peer solidarity and the cult of masculinity

The role of the police service as the peacekeeper in times of violence and unrest, lies at the heart of the service's daily round. The need for peer solidarity and keeping strong for one another is never more important than in those dangerous and critical operations in apprehending criminals or dealing with potentially violent situations. The presence of a 'beat bobby' was and still is a symbol of that safety and security.

Brown and Campbell (1994: 151), citing research findings of Fielding (1987), describe the policeman as confronted with two mythic images: (a) the force as 'a crime- and disorder-controlling, mission orientated, dispassionate and tough body of men', and (b) the other of policewomen 'who are weak, emotional, sympathetic and service orientated'. Indeed one researcher Martin (1989) concluded that sexism and opposition to women officers was crucial for men to maintain their own occupational identities. Such powerful attitudes impact on client work, especially with women.

Keeping strong and a cool head, and managing crises effect-ively, are all part of the expected daily armoury of police officers. Anticipating danger and dealing with it defines their role. For many clients who are police officers, making an appointment is counter-cultural in the face of having to keep strong. Once in the room, the counsellor is requested not to keep records or to see them (the clients) in alternative locations.

Getting started may be a protracted process as clients both test the counsellor's strength to cope with their distress, and begin to overcome their reticence in revealing problems which they per-ceive as a sign of weakness. Clients may fear that they are psychologically unfit for work, that they may have their firearm temporarily removed, or that their peers might know. Counsel-ling, for them, entails a considerable loss of face and runs counter to their image of themselves as police officers.

Supervisees demonstrate having to keep strong for their clients, often being faced with heart-wrenching stories of human misery such as shootings, abuse of children, or daily disasters. The transferred pressure to get their clients back to work is consider-able. Keeping strong affects women officers in a slightly different manner. Often, they are perceived by their male counterparts as weak, are ridiculed, and as a result give themselves a hard time for not fulfilling the male stereotype of the strong, omnipotent officer.

Thus, counsellors are faced with transferential issues – are they strong enough to contain the pain of the client? Will the 'parent' counsellor ridicule or criticize them for being weak and vulner-able? Will the organization criticize them for letting it down by being unfit? Often counsellors are confronted with the anger of the client against the police service which the client perceives to be the cause of their distress, whether through trauma, dis-ciplinary matters or otherwise. Clients experiencing the pain of broken intimate relationships may invite erotic transference with their counsellor.

One supervisee reported feeling at her wits' end from the unrelenting pressure, in and out of sessions, from one female officer who had been involved in a traumatic incident. The counsellor asked in supervision whether she should offer the officer two sessions a week. Could she have some help with a list of desensitization techniques which might speed up the healing process to enable her client to get back to work as quickly as possible? This pressure was unconsciously assimilated by this

supervisor who found himself seduced into rescuing the supervisee only to be challenged in his own supervision!

Working with the supervisee's countertransference is paramount – erotic transference, identifying and raising awareness
about the source of a supervisee's tiredness, anger, rescuing;
enabling the supervisee to experience their vulnerability; and
giving permission not to be strong. The organization impacts
counter-transferentially on the supervision process as counsellors
grapple with their confusion over their multiplicity of roles: their
attempt to go the 'extra mile'; their response to organizational
hype around managing trauma – in short, to be and perform like
Atlas!

This supervisor has experienced the exhaustion, frustration, and
temptation to be like Atlas, to provide solutions and be the strong,
secure one for the projected weak supervisee – yet another
example of a parallel process of the organizational system re-
capitulated in supervision. What ample testimony for the importance of regular professional supervision where my consultant
supervisor can be strong enough for me to hold my own pro-
jective needs!

Crisis and trauma

Jermier, Gaines and McIntosh (1989), in analysing reactions to
physically dangerous work, pointed out that it was the anticipation of danger that fed the notion that police officers needed
physical strength for fighting crime, and attending to human
disaster and misery. Traumatic incidents have come to symbolize
the intensity of police work in the 1990s.

As a consequence there is a highly organized response programme to support officers involved in such incidents. Cynics
point out that the service is acutely aware of the potential threat of
litigation, as, for example, in the Hillsborough Case. This hides an
evident truth within the service that human life is of value, and
one which traditionally it has acted on with great compassion
over the years. Clients present traumas often as a result of current
incidents which trigger unresolved distress from previous incidents or losses in earlier employment, for example in the Forces.

Given 'the cult of masculinity', male officers are often loath to
submit to psychological debriefing or counselling with the result

that Post-Traumatic Stress Disorder (PTSD) may arise at a later date. Counsellors and other colleagues are regularly rostered to act as psychological debriefers. As a result, appointments with clients are changed at short notice, counsellors work more hours (having already completed a full day's caseload), and safety issues such as supervision and their own need for debriefing are neglected.

Diagnosis for PTSD can be complicated when there are associated symptoms such as depression or anxiety disorders (Scott and Stradling 1992). As a result supervisees present anxiety about counselling such clients. Should they seek a referral? What progress is possible in time-limited interventions such as six sessions? What techniques are useful? Which orientation is most suitable? As differing views emerge from research, so does confusion for counsellors and service managers alike.

The supervisor can encourage the supervisee to use her strengths of assessment by clarifying organizational protocols and therapeutic interventions. Trauma contributes to the counsellors' countertransferences, for example they become tired, exhausted, lack concentration, experience anger at the perpetrators of violence and the organization, and want to rescue the client from further upset.

An experienced supervisee questioned her ability to work with a client presenting with Post-Traumatic Stress symptoms. She felt unsafe as she imagined the wrath of management if she misdiagnosed. Her view of the organization as critical parent coupled with her felt sense of organizational hype around managing trauma, undermined her confidence and competence. Others have shared feelings of competitiveness with each other in being 'successful' with clients working with traumatic stress.

Training, acquiring psychological knowledge, and being aware of current research are important for counsellors and supervisors alike to keep themselves up to date. Assisting supervisees to monitor the personal safety of officers suffering from PTS is good practice, although research shows UK police officers have lower suicide rates than men in other occupational groups (Office of Population Census and Surveys 1988).

Following a particularly pressurized day of supervising, this supervisor remarked how tired, lacking in concentration, tetchy, and disorientated he felt. His own consultant supervisor reflected that she was witnessing in him symptoms of PTS mirroring those within the organizational supervisory context!

Good versus evil

The history of the police is one of regulation between the forces of good and evil – expressed in stories of 'cops and robbers'. The close association of the police with promoting good and fighting evil has always been evident. Kleinig (1996) provides a useful suggestion in his demand to evaluate the work of the police in terms of the moral outcomes, rather than on the unrealistic expectation that police officers will exercise a strict code of personal morality at all times. In working with clients, it is common for them to use 'splitting' and 'scapegoating'. In cases where clients are victimized by the organization, for example through bullying or suspension, both client and counsellor wrestle with the idealization of the forces of good and evil projected on to them.

Both Morgan (1986) and Egan (1994) direct attention to how forces of the 'shadow' impact on all levels of organizational life. Supervisees have described feelings of horror and fear in the face of stories of hate, abuse, exploitation, annihilation. They have shared their existential angst as counsellors – that feeling of being faceless, voiceless, impotent, and non-existent as the shadowy forces of the organization corporately undermine their confidence and competence.

The temptation for the supervisor is to be pulled into the split (Carroll 1996b) by siding with the forces of good, for example encouraging expressions of anger against the perpetrators of exploitation, bullying and harassment; and against the criminal actions of those who shoot and stab and maim police personnel. Again, this may be evidenced in the counter-transferential feelings of the supervisee and the supervisor through the experience of parallel process.

One supervisee constantly referred to her work with a depressed client as doomed. The counsellor's sense of doom and despondency was intensified as the client went through a catalogue of personal tragedies – sexual abuse, family deaths, a traumatic incident at work. The counsellor's anger was further exacerbated by the organization's inability to act tolerantly with her client. The experience of the supervisor is often one of containment of this struggle between the forces of good and evil in the client and the supervisee. In one sense the supervisor symbolically acts as a 'psychological priest', 'shaman' or 'Merlin' who contains the disparate parts of client, organization and supervisee.

A significant client group is that of suspended officers – those undergoing investigation by the Criminal Investigation Bureau or who are awaiting the outcome of internal disciplinary boards, or criminal court cases. The organization treats them as virtually 'guilty until found innocent'. Counsellors are faced with severely depressed and sometimes suicidal clients, and are required to 'hold' them psychologically for periods up to eighteen months. One supervisee psychologically supported one of these clients through three court retrials. The client's sense of despair was almost intolerable as was the exhaustion of the counsellor in containing the client through this experience.

Holding the 'counter-cultural flow' can be exhausting for counsellor and supervisor. The creation of spaces becomes an essential part of counsellor and supervisor health, for example having adequate time off, allowing spaces in the diary between client appointments, undertaking alternative activities, and reducing case-loads.

Accelerated change (achievement versus paternalism)

The welfare tradition of the Police Service was the cradle from which psychological services emerged. The care which the police extend to their peers and their dependants through financial assistance and practical support is impressive, especially in times of bereavement and illness.

The counsellor as 'pastor' makes home visits to those officers who are temporarily incapacitated and unable to visit the counselling room. However, this practice is questioned as an appropriate service for the 1990s in terms of the best use of time, issues of health and safety and an increasing professionalism on the part of practitioners. This is but one example of how the professionalization of services challenges the traditional forms of paternalism within the counselling service itself.

Policing has undergone major change in the past 20 years, and recently by the implementation of the Sheehey Report (HMSO 1993) which emphasizes the de-layering of certain ranks within the service, contractual work, greater flexibility of movement of personnel and a more skilled and professionalized service. What is often neglected is the management of the individual in adjusting to the organizational changes (Horsted and Doherty 1994) when sickness and demoralization may result.

Many police officers, while welcoming and embracing a more efficient service, face crises of identity in respect of their traditional role. The notion of 'a professional police manager' emerged in the 1960s and 1970s at a time when the status of senior officers was seen to be under threat. Increased paperwork is a major cause of frustration and stress (Brown and Campbell 1994). The acceleration of technology has necessitated the rapid increase of specialized expertise.

Brown and Campbell (1994: 149), reporting on research about change in the police, comment:

> social changes will occur only when irresistible and more powerful forces are brought to bear from outside. . . . maintaining the status quo is to a degree a game played between the police and those outside forces, but also within the organization itself.

Counsellors in supervision report on the impact of change on their clients and themselves. Change and specialization of roles place great strain on some of the longer-serving officers. A typical challenge for the counsellor is to distinguish between the genuine distress of some clients, and those conscious and unconscious attempts by others to use counselling as a means to convince the Chief Medical Officer of their unsuitability for continued service.

This difficulty is often exacerbated by the involvement of a number of health professionals such as doctors, psychiatrists, counsellors, as they are variously played off against each other by the client. Here, the role of the supervisor is to assist the supervisee to separate out the contractual agreements between him- or herself, other professionals and the client. Uncertainties about the boundaries of confidentiality emerge as the client moves between the health professionals without communicating this movement to all concerned. The cost is considerable to the organization in terms of finance, upset and wasted valuable professional time.

Ideally, supervision at all levels in the organization could greatly assist the effective management and resolution of these kinds of issues. The temptation is immense for the organization to scapegoat any one of the professionals involved (Hawkins and Shohet 1989). From time to time it is the counsellor who becomes the unwitting victim of internal criticism from fellow professionals.

In assisting supervisees to help clients manage the effects of change, the supervisor is frequently:

- holding the needs of the supervisee as part of a changing organization, and its impact on the counselling process;
- helping to manage manipulation by client and organization;
- helping the counsellor be clear about the impact of organizational pressure resulting from the uncoordinated networking of involved professionals.

The result for the supervisee is an experience like 'plaiting fog', that is, trying to hold together the different strands in a unified whole – and holding the tension between the needs of client, counsellor and organization.

In helping officers manage the impact of organizational change and its consequent internal transition, counsellors get caught up in their own organizational process of change. At times the focus of supervision is on what is manageable in the short term, for example concentrating on work with clients. At other times, the focus is the empowerment of the counsellor in addressing difficulties as a result of change within the counselling service. Counsellors express feeling a lack of competence in working with their clients, and question their motivation for working with the organization. Their distress will sometimes be expressed in forms of 'collegiate abuse', feelings of insecurity, and protestations of anger with management. This experience can be replicated as a form of parallel process in their work with clients.

The power of uniform, hierarchy and rank

It seems self-evident that rank, uniform and hierarchy pervade all aspects of police culture. As in other uniformed organizations, especially the Armed Forces, the notion that external authority is necessary for internal discipline and order is central.

Those in middle management, for example sergeants, tend to experience high levels of stress, as they face pressure from senior management from above and operational demands from below (Brown and Campbell 1994). With the de-layering of some senior ranks this has meant increased pressure and workloads for such managers. With the decrease in the number of ranks, career progression has been curtailed. There is increased competition for senior officer posts, partly influenced by an increased intake of 'graduate' recruits and the extended use of civilians.

There is little research to support the notion that uniformed organizations attract particular personality types. The hierarchical, authoritarian, rank-conscious culture does produce identifiable behaviour which contributes to stress caused by bullying, and different forms of aggression and harassment. Davidson and Veno (1980), using Jung's development of personality types (Stevens 1990), discovered that extroverts were more stable than introverts when in potentially dangerous situations. Kirmeyer and Diamond (1985) found the police force included more ' "A" Type personalities' than in the general population.

Experience attests that there is a significant sample of clients who tend towards an 'anti-social personality adaptation' (Ware 1983). This has many positive aspects – a capacity to outwit the criminal, aggressiveness, the ability to think well on one's feet. However, at times of trauma and negative stress, destructive forces can be released that are difficult to manage both at work and home. Perhaps this illustrates the unconscious need of some such individuals to contain the destructive potential within a structured disciplined environment for creative and purposeful activity. Working with such clients can be a challenge for counsellors who report feeling manipulated, sometimes bullied and at other times charmed! The difference between the personality types of counsellors, supervisors and police service clients can easily create conflictual and adversarial structures in counselling and supervision. Supervisor and counsellor can collude unconsciously to outwit the client; or devalue the client's issues in order to feel superior; or try to change the primary structure of the client's personality to be more in keeping with their own, thus reducing their own discomfort.

Organizationally, managers in the field will attempt to pull rank by asking for confidential information about clients. Counsellors report feeling under pressure to 'perform' well with clients (be successful) especially when seeing clients referred by high-ranking officers. This pressure is unconsciously passed on by incidental enquiries and comments of internal service managers.

One supervisee commented, 'But she's only a civilian . . .', mirroring the felt divide in status between civilians and officers in the service. Clearly the counsellor felt some status in dealing with an officer rather than with a civilian!

Wrestling with the application of equal opportunities

Workplace bullying and harassment as a growing feature of working life (Adams 1992) unfolds all too frequently in the counselling room. For the supervisor, containing the anger of supervisees and their sense of impotence at not making a difference with their clients, is common. For many clients, the counsellor is one of the first people who has understood their situation. The transferential relationship of ally is powerful for client and counsellor. Frequently supervisors' priorities are managing the counter-transferential feelings of the supervisee, helping them to manage their sense of impotence about changing the organization of which they are a part, and being a sufficient container for the pain of the client. It is a temptation for those who have been in the service some years not to acknowledge the immense distress bullying and harassment can cause.

Counsellors are faced with woman clients who have suffered sexual harassment and live in constant fear that making an official complaint will result in reprisals, lengthy proceedings and ostracization by peers.

In a group supervision session (one male and three female supervisees with a male supervisor), the male supervisee presented his work with a male officer who had been disciplined for alleged sexual harassment of a female officer. At the end of the session the supervisor supportively touched the male counsellor's arm. This triggered an attack by the female supervisees who felt that the supervisor had not sufficiently acknowledged the plight of the victim of the harassment. The potency of this emotive issue resulted in a review of roles, the purpose of supervision and the nature of the interpersonal relationships within the group. This raised the following questions:

- Was the supervisor identified by the women in the group with the perpetrator?
- Were the males of the group actively ignoring the plight of the female victim?
- Was the supervisor somehow being seen to use his rank (power) visibly to support the only other male in the group, implicitly ignoring, and hence, further abusing the female victim?

The challenge for supervisors in this context is their ability to be flexible in focusing and re-focusing their lenses at any one time on the relationship between counsellor and client, the relationship between counsellor and the organizational third parties, the relationship between supervisor and counsellor and between supervisor and organization, and, at a fantasy level, between supervisor and client – like the six-eyed supervisor of Hawkins and Shohet (1989), plus an organizational eye. The view is always panoramic and systemic. As the organizational culture of the Police Service impacts on all the participants of counselling and supervision, the role of the supervisor is like that of a conductor of an orchestra enabling the counsellor to distinguish and work with the melody of the client from the harmonies and disharmonies of the other players.

Case study demonstrating the impact of culture on supervision

The case will provide initial client details and the nature of referral and initial assessment, and the impact of organizational culture will be traced as it affected the counselling and supervisory processes.

Harry is 52, a serving Police Officer of over 30 years who recently changed job through his inability to perform 'front-line duties'. Encouraged by his family, he referred himself for counselling following increasing outbursts of anger.

In the first session, among a catalogue of losses, he spoke of witnessing a particularly gruesome incident in which he had dragged mutilated bodies out of a train accident some ten years previously, the images and sensations of which continued to live with him daily.

After an initial assessment session the counsellor agreed to see him for up to 12 sessions. Post-Traumatic Stress and depressive symptoms were identified. Scores on Hammerberg's Penn Inventory and Beck's Depression Inventory, while high, did not show sufficient severity to indicate Post-Traumatic Stress Disorder or severe depression. The counsellor presented the client in supervision four times throughout the period of counselling.

Needing to keep strong

The counsellor experienced the client as being very defended and unaware of the impact of the multiple losses he had experienced (own child, parents, relatives, his job, his self-esteem) and of the traumatic incident – 'I don't know what grieving is.' As a serving officer the need for strength in crisis was what was expected. He did not attend a psychological debriefing. He had attended counselling for depression.

Supervision focused on the counsellor's despondency at not being able to make an empathic link with the client, or work with the client's low self-esteem. The racket system (Erskine and Zalcman 1979) was used as a way of helping the counsellor understand her counter-transferential feelings of incompetence in working with depressed clients – 'I'm a useless counsellor who cannot communicate effectively with this client; it's my fault.' The counsellor was helped to own the degree of challenge and difficulty which the client presented, to recognize the source of the client's distress, and the client's lack of ability to express feelings.

Trauma and 'getting it right'

The counsellor felt she had to make a successful outcome for the organization, and felt pressure to 'get it right'. It was noted that the counsellor 'held back' in bringing the client to supervision until session five. The counsellor also experienced the uncertainty of protocols in the area of managing trauma. After 12 sessions the client was referred outside the organization for further psychological help.

The supervisor's role focused on encouraging the counsellor to use external assessment instruments as a way of supporting the counsellor's assessment; to remind the counsellor of the impact of so many losses; and on the counsellor's ability in working with the same.

Managing change in individual and organization

The client had been forced to change his role from front-line duties to a more maintenance role with considerable loss of status. Further, his loss of self-esteem had been intensified by his close colleague's promotion.

The supervisor reminded the supervisee of the possible impact on her of internal changes to the counselling service. He helped her to explore the perceived and felt pressure to deliver a 'successful' outcome for client and organization. Totton (1997) gives timely warning that counsellors need to be aware of how the system of the organization does change the counsellor, however much he or she tries to stem the counter-cultural tide.

The counsellor as 'expert'

The client came to counselling expecting the counsellor to work magic. The magic for this client was to provide answers to his dilemmas – 'What's life about? I don't know any more.' 'Tell me what I have to do. . . .'

For the client, the counsellor was the organizational 'expert'. In an organization that administers the laws, rules and regulations for the correct ordering of society, his expectation was that there were similar ones for the ordering of human life.

In supervision the counsellor presented as being ignorant about the nature of loss and PTS symptomology, about making contact, and about the skills and techniques which would work with this client. Initially the supervisor sat there also asking himself the same questions. The supervisee projected on to the supervisor the idealized counsellor and disempowered herself in the process – another example of 'parallel process', mirroring the client's expectation of the counsellor and organization as experts, and the counsellor's expectation of the supervisor as expert.

Good versus evil

The client was experiencing existential angst as he wrestled with the meaning of good and evil in his life – and tried to make sense of what the future held for him. The counsellor had checked out the client's potential for self-harm. Harry's experience of reunion with a loved one during the period of the counselling gave him hope expressed in his statement, 'When I met him it was like returning to a time of innocence.' If his 'God' seemed to have abandoned him, he checked that his counsellor had not – 'Do you think about me between sessions?' The counsellor was both moved and felt the weight of responsibility for the client.

Supervision was a time when the weight was shared and where the supervisor could help the supervisee test the reality of her significant contribution to the client's progress. The process was humbling both for supervisee and supervisor.

In an evaluation session with the supervisor, the counsellor commented:

> You helped me specifically gain a focus amongst a lot of information, and enabled me to move forward – I felt motivated as my 'over-whelmedness' decreased.

> I felt supported in the suggestion to use the Beck D.I. and the Penn Inventory.

> You held a helicopter view for me.

> I experienced your support, empathy and guidance.

> You allowed me to develop my own sense-making and own strategies in working with my perception of this client, i.e. test reality.

> You helped me check out and hold the ethical boundaries – especially around my doubts about the client self-harming.

> I felt your lively engagement in supervision and interest in my client.

> I appreciate your coaxing me through a very challenging client.

Training case study

The following case study will highlight some of the issues faced by counsellors and supervisors within the Police setting.

Dave, a 40-year-old Police Officer is on a disciplinary sus-pension following a motor cycle accident while on duty, which resulted in the serious injury of a young pedestrian. Dave has been married twice, and has children from both marriages. He keeps mentioning the lack of contact with his first two children who are 12 and 15 years old. He has had a series of affairs, and says his wife does not love him.

In session two, he disclosed that he had been constantly abused between the ages of 6 and 11 by a close family friend, and that he thinks about it a lot. He says rather stoically, that while he understands that the organization has to discipline him, they are scapegoating him by raising grievances from his past. He says he wants to 'get out' but knows that the disciplinary could go on for up to a year. He is currently experiencing financial difficulties and being investigated by the Child Support Agency. To the counsellor, he seems very shut off from his feelings.

The counselling organization will provide up to six sessions with review, and the possibility of a further six if the service managers approve the counsellor's request. The counselling service will provide a 'befriending relationship' during the period of his suspension. The counsellor comes to supervision feeling overwhelmed by the client's situation.

Recommendations for the training of supervisors

To the six domains of training by Carroll (1996b: 32), must be added understanding and working with the organizational dimension. The different models of supervision, together with clinical issues such as working with time-limited interventions, crisis management and working across different orientations, have been extensively documented in the literature. Here, the focus is on those organizational aspects which provide the contextual framework within which supervision takes place. While the following suggestions are by no means exhaustive, they are offered for serious attention by trainers in this field.

Contracting

The Three-Cornered Contract (English 1975; Hay 1992; Towler 1996) and the Clinical Rhombus (Ekstein and Wallerstein 1976), both with their notions of 'equidistance' or 'psychological distance', are models which focus students' attention on the significance of accountability and potential distortions in the organizational context.

Experience highlights the essential nature of contracting with the organization as well as with the supervisee, a process mirrored in setting up counselling contracts. Managing a multiplicity of clients (Towler 1996) can be a confusing, exhausting and confidence-denting experience for supervisor and supervisee. Inskipp and Proctor (1993), Proctor (1997), Feltham and Dryden (1994), Carroll (1996b), Shea and Bond (1997), BAC (1995) and others provide informative practical frameworks for reflection on issues of contracting and maintaining professional boundaries.

Parallel process

The literature and understanding of the fractal phenomenon of 'parallel process' as experienced in one-to-one encounters and within the organizational context, is explored comprehensively by Carroll (1996b: 103–8, 120). As a feature of the supervision process, its relation to the organization, its culture and the individual counsellor has to be managed carefully – and not overused.

Organizational dynamics

Understanding the dynamics of organizations provides the supervisor with a working handle on unconscious processes which impact on the supervision process. Morgan's (1986) eloquent exposition of organization as 'psychic prison'; the work of Bion (1961), Menzies (1990), Obholzer and Roberts (1994), Hawkins and Shohet (1989), Egan (1994), Clarkson and Pokorny (1994) on exploring the psychodynamics of organizations; and Critchley and Casey (1989) and Berne (1963) on humanistic perspectives are all worth a serious visit.

Organizational culture

The literature on culture is a growth industry. The work of Hawkins (1997) at the Bath Consultancy Group provides a rich store of experience and a current critique of existing literature and research in this field. His article 'Organizational culture: sailing betwen evangelism and complexity' is written with this dual focus, and provides an excellent bibliography. Mapping the organizational culture with counsellors is both a rewarding exercise, and invaluable resource for supervisor and counsellors alike.

In-house organizational material

Last but not least, is the importance of supervisors familiarizing themselves with organizational protocols and procedures which impact on the lives of clients and supervisees alike. Organizational newssheets and in-house magazines provide a feel for the changing nature and culture of the organization.

Conclusion

Having traced the impact of some cultural characteristics of one uniformed organization on supervision, it may be tempting to believe that the experience is general. This highlights the necessity for supervisors to discern the particular cultural characteristics of the organization. To be aware of the potential and actual influence of conscious and unconscious process within an organization can greatly assist clarity in the process of supervision. The supervisor is pulled in all directions – by counsellor, client and organization. Good practice emerges in being able to hold the tension between them all.

There is no substitute for 'learning by doing' in this work. This chapter is written in appreciation of all the supervisees and associated professionals who have greatly assisted my professional development in this organization. Finally, my thanks go to two Christines, my partner and my own supervisor, who have given me such unfailing support in my work.

References

Adams, A. (1992) *Bullying at Work: How to Confront and Overcome It*. London: Virago.

BAC (1995) *Code of Ethics and Practice for Supervisors of Counsellors*. Rugby: British Association for Counselling.

Berne, E. (1963) *The Structure and Dynamics of Organizations and Groups*. New York: Grove Press, Inc.

Bion, W.R. (1961) *Experiences in Groups*. London: Tavistock Publications.

Brown, J.M. and Campbell, E.A. (1994) *Stress and Policing: Sources and Strategies*. Chichester: Wiley.

Carroll, M. (1996a) *Counselling Supervision: Theory, Skills and Practice*. London: Cassell.

Carroll, M. (1996b) *Workplace Counselling*. London: Sage.

Clarkson, P. (1995) *The Therapeutic Relationship in Psychoanalysis, Counselling Psychology and Psychotherapy*. London: Whurr.

Clarkson, P. and Pokorny, M. (eds) (1994) *Handbook of Psychotherapy*. London: Routledge.

Crandell, R. and Allen, R.D. (1982) 'The organizational context of helping relationships', in T.A. Wills (ed.) *Basic Processes in Helping Relationships*. London: Academic Press.

Critchley, B. and Casey, D. (1989) 'Organizations get stuck too', *Leadership and Organization Development Journal*, 10 (4): 3–12.

Davidson, M.J. and Veno, A. (1980) 'Stress and the policeman', in C.L. Cooper and J. Marshall (eds) *White Collar and Professional Stress*. Chichester: Wiley & Sons.

de Shazer, S. (1985) *Keys to Solution in Brief Therapy*. London and New York: W.W. Norton & Co.

Egan, G. (1994) *Working the Shadow-Side: A Guide to Positive Behind-the-Scenes Management*. San Francisco, CA: Jossey-Bass.

Ekstein, R. and Wallerstein, R.S. (1976) *The Teaching and Learning of Psychotherapy*. New York: International.

English, F. (1975) 'The three-cornered contract', *Transactional Analysis Journal*, 5 (4): 383–4.

Erskine, R. and Zalcman, M. (1979) 'The racket system: a model for racket analysis', *Transactional Analysis Journal*, 9 (1): 51–9.

Feltham, C. and Dryden, W. (1994) *Developing Counsellor Supervision*. London: Sage.

Fielding, N. (1987) *Joining Forces*, London: Routledge.

Gleick, J. (1988) *Chaos: Making a New Science*. London: Heinemann.

Handy, C. (1993) *Understanding Organizations* (4th edn). Harmondsworth: Penguin.

Harrison, R. (1972) 'How to describe your organization', *Harvard Business Review*, 50 (23): 119–28.

Hawkins, P. (1997) 'Organizational culture: sailing between evangelism and complexity', *Human Relations*, 50 (4): 417–44.

Hawkins, P. and Shohet, R. (1989) *Supervision in the Helping Professions*, Buckingham: Open University Press.

Hay, J. (1992) *Transactional Analysis for Trainers*. London: McGraw-Hill.

HMSO (1993) *The Sheehey Report: Inquiry into Police Responsibilities and Review*. London: HMSO.

Holloway, E. (1995) *Clinical Supervision: A Systems Approach*. Thousand Oaks, CA: Sage.

Horsted, J. and Doherty, N. (1994) 'Poles apart? – integrating business process redesign and human resource management', *Business Change and Re-engineering*, 1 (4): 49–56.

Inskipp, F. and Proctor, B. (1993) *Making the Most of Supervision*. Part 1. Twickenham, Middlesex: Cascade Publications.

Jermier, J.M., Gaines, J. and McIntosh, N.J. (1989) 'Reactions to physically dangerous work: a conceptual and empirical analysis', *Journal of Organizational Behaviour*, 10 (15): 15–33.

Kets de Vries, F.R. and Miller, D. (1984) *The Neurotic Organization*. San Francisco, CA: Jossey-Bass.

Kirmeyer, S. and Diamond, A. (1985) 'Coping by police officers: a study of role and stress type A and type B behaviour patterns', *Journal of Occupational Behaviour*, 6: 1883–5.

Kleinig, J. (1996) *The Ethics of Policing*. Cambridge: Cambridge University Press.

Martin, S.E. (1989) 'Women and policing: the 80s and beyond', in D.J. Kennedy (ed.) *Police and Policing: Contemporary Issues*. New York: Praeger.

Menzies, I. (1990) 'Social systems as a defence against anxiety; an empirical study of the nursing service of a general hospital', in E. Trist and H. Murray (eds) *The Social Engagement of Social Science*, Vol. 1: *The Socio-psychological Perspective*. London: Free Association Books.

Morgan, G. (1986) *Images of Organization*. London: Sage.

Obholzer, A. and Roberts, V.Z. (1994) *The Unconscious at Work: Individual and Organizational Stress in Human Services*. London: Routledge.

Office of Population Census and Surveys (1988) *Occupational Mortality*. Series DS No. 6. London: HMSO.

Proctor, B. (1997) 'Supervision for counsellors in organizations', in M. Carroll and M. Walton (eds) *The Handbook of Counselling in Organizations*. London: Sage.

Randall, R., Southgate, J. and Tomlinson, F. (1980) *Cooperative and Community Group Dynamics*. London: Barefoot Books.

Scott, M.J. and Stradling, S.G. (1992) *Counselling for Post-Traumatic Stress Disorder*. London: Sage.

Shea, C. and Bond, T. (1997) 'Ethical issues for counselling in organizations', in M. Carroll and M. Walton (eds) *The Handbook of Counselling in Organizations*. London: Sage.

Stevens, A. (1990) *On Jung*. Harmondsworth: Penguin.

Totton, M. (1997) 'Inputs and outcomes: the medical model and professionalism', *Self and Society – A Journal of Humanistic Psychology*, 25 (4): 3–8.

Towler, J. (1996) 'Supervision and culture', Roehampton Training and Consultancy Update. Roehampton Institute.

———— (1997) 'Managing the counselling process in organizations', in M. Carroll and M. Walton (eds) *The Handbook of Counselling in Organizations*. London: Sage.

Ware, P. (1983) 'Personality adaptations', *Transactional Analysis Journal*, 13 (1): 11–19.

Index

Lee-Borden, N., 30
Lees, J., 94, 95, 97
Lesser, R.M., 162
Lethem, J., 95
Levant, R., 25, 26
Levinson, D.J., 166
liaison, 91, 97
Lichtenberg, J.W., 26
limits, 85, 97
Littrell, J.M., 30, 131
Loftus, S.J., 168
Loganbill, C., 131
Lorenz, J., 30

Makin, T., 38–9, 50
Malley, M., 61
Marsella, A., 64
Martin, L., 142
Martin, S.E., 182
Mathers, N., 96
Maylon, A., 55
McCabe, M.P., 170
McLeod, J., 161
McNeill, B.W., 132
Mearns, D., 93
medical services, 105, 110, 113, 117, 118
mentoring, 87
Menzies, I., 196
Messing, A.E., 62
Meyer, J.K., 57
Miller, H.M.L., 160–1
Milton, M., 77
mind-body, 86
ministers, 160, 167, 169
Morgan, G., 178, 186, 196
Morin, S., 55, 59
Moulds, J.D., 170
multi-disciplinary team, 85, 91–3, 99
Murphy, A., 96

narratives, 87
Neal, C., 69
Nelson, M.L., 29, 30, 31
Neufeldt, S.A., 132
Newton, F.B.,
Nias, J., 92

Obholzer, A., 196
O'Connell, B., 92

Office of Population Census and
    Surveys, 185
O'Neill, J.M., 25
Orbach, S., 98
organizations,
    conscious/unconscious sides, 198
    counter-culture of, 181, 183, 187, 194
    countertransference of, 184
    culture of, 178–180, 192, 197
    dynamics of, 188, 197
    management of change in, 199–9
    shadow-side of, 147, 186
    and supervision, 141
    types of, 178
organizational,
    change, 141
    contexts, 3
    culture, 148
    issues, 111–13

Page, S., 144
parallel process, 98, 144, 151, 180–1,
    184, 185, 189, 194, 196
Pedersen, P., 13, 64
Pengelly, P., 92
Pilgrim, D., 2
Pleck, J., 25
Pokorny, M., 196
police,
    cult of masculinity, 178, 183, 184, 191
    culture of, 178
    equal opportunities, 179, 182, 186,
        190, 191
    ethics and, 179, 186, 194
    hierarchy, 179, 189, 190
    objectives of, 178
    peer solidarity of, 178, 182
    professionalism of, 187
    trauma and, 178, 183, 184, 192–4
    and uniform, 179, 189–90
    welfare and counselling tradition,
        187
Polkinghorne, D.E., 26
Pollack, W.S., 25
Ponterotto, J., 13, 19
power, 64
priests, 162, 166–7
    and celibacy, 162, 167
    diocesan, 165